MORE THAN
HUMAN

THE VALUE OF CULTIVATING THE
HUMAN SPIRIT IN YOUR ORGANIZATION

BILL PROTZMANN

MUSIC CARE INC.

The best leaders are the ones who know how to tap into the human spirit. First, their own. Then, the spirit of those they care for and serve. In *More Than Human*, Bill Protzmann explores practical and actionable ways we can bring spirituality into the workplace including best practices of respect, kindness, dignity and sustainability. I recommend this book to everyone who wants to grow as a wholehearted leader.

—Kevin Kruse, New York Times Bestselling Author, *Employee Engagement 2.0*

This book is a structured response to the craziness that overtakes so many of us these days, set in the form of a best-practices handbook for organizations. Organizations of any size can benefit from this succinct, hands-on approach to re-engaging their collective human spirit.

Colonel David W. Sutherland, US Army (Ret.)
President, Sutherland Partnership, Inc.

MORE THAN HUMAN
The Value of Cultivating the Human Spirit in Your Organization
BY BILL PROTZMANN

Published by
MUSIC CARE INC., San Diego, CA

Published in
collaboration with

LAMP POST inc.
www.lamppostpublishers.com

ISBN-13: 978-069290-074-1 (Hard Cover)

...you are not only good, but also the cause of goodness in others.

— SOCRATES

CONTENTS

Have you noticed how many books these days start out with a message from the attorneys? "Your results may vary," or "these statements have not been reviewed by a physician," or, my personal favorite, which leads off quite a few books about how to do things better or be more healthy: "no one in any way remotely connected with this book or otherwise assumes responsibility for anything written here, nor shall any of those people or institutions, their significant others, their lawyers, or their pets be liable for errors, omissions, or use of this information for any purpose, including direct, indirect, punitive, incidental, special or consequential damage arising out of or in any way connected with the use of the information in this book."

Have you also noticed how many how-to and self-help books – like this one – are often backed by years of research, extensively footnoted, and sometimes peer-reviewed?

Isn't it about time we thought more carefully about all that?

Shouldn't books, especially self-help ones, offer ideas and guidance that you can prove for yourself? Isn't it about time writers encouraged readers to do something that many of us have forgotten to do at all: think for ourselves?

Research and inquiry are a big part of how we advance sustainable ideas in the 21st Century. I've no issue with that in general: well-substantiated ideas are much better than educated guesses should there be an option between the two, but there's a more fundamental and ageless concept at work in this book.

The ideas presented here aren't new. Many of them are ancient. If you aren't familiar with the wisdom literature in which they're based, the Internet makes it easy to do your own research; this book would be thousands of pages long if I did it for you. For that reason, I've kept the footnotes to a minimum. If you're interested, it just doesn't take that much effort to find out for yourself that the ideas we'll discuss together actually work. People and organizations use these ideas more and more, so perhaps that renewed interest brought you to this book.

Ask yourself: if given the choice between a scientific peer-reviewed study of several thousand "subjects" getting measurable results from a particular way of behaving, or knowing simply through your own personal experience that behaving a certain way produces an expected result, would you wait for the science before adopting the behavior?

This book is an opportunity to remind yourself and your organization of behaviors that work, and work well. The choice is yours. If you need to wait for the science – and the inevitable disclaimer that will accompany it – stop reading right now. Or, you can jump in and start doing this stuff.

Still reading? Want to move ahead? Welcome aboard. From here on, it's all on *you*.

MORE THAN
HUMAN

CHAPTER ONE

INTRODUCTION

We are talking about the human spirit. *Your* human spirit and its power in your organization.

What drives you…hard? Do you fall for success…hard?

Do you dare to do ordinary things in an extraordinary way? Do you want to? Why and how would you do that?

If you're reading this, you are already connected to your human spirit. You can use that.

Whether your human spirit is hard charging and lit up or barely warm enough to keep you from icing over, the "something more about life-ness" is what we're going to discuss. That somethingness might be fierce, courageous, and daring, or subtle, steely, and calm. It can be a paradox of the brash and bold alongside the quiet and compelling. Even if it feels like your interior embers glow red or burn out, in this book, that "human spirit" is what we call "spirituality."

And that's where it gets real.

The practice of human spirit.

Practical spirituality.

So, to put it to work in your organization, this book is about spiritual best practices, which, by the way, have contagious acceptance, unlimited scalability, and tremendous value...starting with You. And along the way there will be examples of contrasting spiritual best and spiritual worst practices so that the difference and results are clear.

Ready? Let's do this! Your human spirit deserves it.

Why spirituality? Isn't there a better, less-charged word? Spirituality could offend people! What do you mean anyway?

These questions are also big reasons to write a book about spiritual best practices for organizations. So, to begin, may we take a moment to think about what we mean by "spirituality," just to start things on the same page?

If you are familiar with terms such as "values-based" or "values-oriented" you have encountered spirituality.

If you've ever used a perfect, politically correct joke to break meeting ice or introduce a very long slide deck, you've used a spiritual best practice.

If you are chronically nice to people, say "thank you" out of habit, or have some of those intrinsically natural "people skills" many of us wish we had, you already know how to use spiritual best practice.

Would you consider the suggestion that it's time we named these skills, abilities, and ways of thinking exactly what they are?

In this book, spirituality is not religion. It's not economics, or politics, or environmentalism, or science, either. This discussion also excludes theology. For that reason (and others!), atheists can be quite spiritual. So can religionists. So can economists, politicians, environmentalists, and scientists. So can businesspeople, tradespeople, volunteers, social workers, and professionals. In fact, anyone can practice spirituality simply by choosing to do so, or perhaps by simply becoming aware of their desire to "discover and realize their spirit, that is, their essential selves."[1] It's easy enough for a child to "discover and realize [its] essential self" but more difficult for most adults, therefore, this book.

Have you ever been kind? Appreciative? Funny? Those are ways to practice spirituality. There are others, of course. Think back: Do you recall moments in your life where something significant took place – something that fed a deep inner place inside you that you keep mostly hidden from the world? Could you have purchased that moment for any amount of money? Did that moment leave anything behind for you to display as a trophy afterward? Were you profoundly moved? There's a good chance you had a moment of spirituality – that you discovered a part of your essential self.

Pursuit of that essential self, or spirit, is an intangible act, isn't it? As with many adventures, from video games to "soul work," the practice of spirituality is intangible. Generally we associate spiritual practices with goodness, that is, the "love" side of the "love versus hate" paradigm. There is some relationship between our feelings or emotions and spirituality, but emotions, understood largely as a chemical change in our physical systems in response to some stimulus, are not in and of themselves spirituality. Our emotions serve as a kind of radar for spirituality, and the feelings we experience when practicing spirituality help us recognize the moment when we discover something new about our essential self.

Moments of spiritual practice can happen around any of the four primary emotions: fear, anger, grief, or joy. Hopefully, you may easily recall a joyous moment of spiritual practice: helping a child learn something new, for example, or showing your significant other appreciation. Grief, when it comes, can also be a moment of spiritual practice when we cry together at the funeral of a loved family member. Fear, while it sounds like a feeling we don't like very much, could be part of the inspiration behind the spiritual practice of saving money for future emergencies or retirement. Even anger can propel a spiritual practice, such as protecting a family or a business from harm. Those types of fear and anger are much different from the horrifying terror and rage that make headlines.

While we can feel both love and fear, they seem different in spite of their chemical similarities. Mostly, we "like" love and "dislike" fear. In the context of this book, the term "spirituality" will carry a good connotation – something that we mostly "like" – and, therefore, the spiritual best practices discussed here are intended to be characteristically good, such as those just described for fear and anger, and to carry a positive inflection and energy.

Organizations that hope to achieve more with less, build authentic teams, solve complex problems with innovation, "right-size" (to use the old term), or reinvent themselves, are all candidates for enhanced spiritual practices. Organizations that already do those things often practice spirituality without making it obvious. So let's make it obvious now.

Yes, there will be "how to" later in this book. Before we get to that, it's vital to remember why we would want to practice spiritually outside of the church or family, so let's begin by getting re-acquainted with the "why" before we continue on to the "how."

WHY SPIRITUALITY IN ORGANIZATIONS MATTERS

Organizations that want to have a positive, sustainable impact have come to realize that the way they conduct themselves *matters more than the widgets or services they provide.* There is a fundamental shift in organizations toward responsible, people-centered values and active practice of "intangibles" such as ethics, respect, and integrity. Organizations recognized as "successful" have a measurable commitment to these principles.

Think of the organizations you know and admire. How different are they from organizations you distrust? Why? Is it because your core values and beliefs are the same or different? Do the people leading those two types of organizations exhibit qualities you admire or despise? Now, thinking of those same organizations, can you answer those same questions, but this time without judgment? It can be very hard to separate our likes and dislikes and the value judgments that go along with them from people and organizations that don't conform to our preferences and passions. Often, attempting to be truly objective is just impossible.

Now, imagine yourself as a member of an organization engaged in doing something you love, working alongside others who feel the same way. This organization aligns with your values and passions and you feel embraced in the work, by your co-workers, and in the "big picture" where your organization makes its contribution. It is a completely satisfactory experience for you and everyone involved. One day, a suggestion rocks your perfect organization: something needs to change so that the organization can respond to a new opportunity. No one in particular actually made the suggestion, it just seems like an obvious way to extend the work and meet a new demand for what you and your teammates can do. The team members you admire so much gradually start to line up on different sides of the suggestion; some prefer one approach and some prefer another. Strong feelings about what's "best" for the organization emerge, and before long there's a new kind of stress in the work that wasn't there before.

This cultural unrest can last for some time as the team or organization sorts through options for a response to the change that feels best to everyone. Consultants are called in; offsite meetings take place; new methods are tried, rejected, changed, tried again, adopted. Some workers choose to leave the team; new workers arrive to accept responsibility. Eventually, when the process is successful, the work of the team or organization to transform itself begins to show positive results. Sometimes, teams and organizations don't or can't survive the transformation, and the enterprise ends. Often, if the core ideas were worthy, such enterprises are reborn in some surprising, novel, or innovative way.

If you've ever lived that scenario in real life there's a good chance you're having some feelings about it right now as you remember what took place. Human beings are built that way: we tend to have long memories of discomfort. Even when the eventual results of that distress turn out fine later on, our emotions remind us of the sometimes-painful journey to reach that new point of satisfaction. We tend to learn well under those conditions, too, and the lessons we can carry away from such an experience often stay with us for life. Those deeply ingrained lessons we've really suffered to learn – the ones that stay with us for life – are the important ones.

This process – challenge to the way things are, followed by foment, followed by a new perspective, followed by a successful realignment of the organization to adapt to that change – can be called "spiritual growth."

Why "spiritual" growth? It's true that teams change physical size, and change mentally/intellectually in terms of the processes they follow, but the notion of spirituality as applied to organizations needs some discussion. While there are certainly physical and mental aspects of change in organizations as they adapt to new opportunities and challenges, it's intriguing that the most successful organizations appear to share a number of intangible attributes beyond their physical and intellectual capabilities. It's important, for example, that human beings feel a sense of positive self worth. Organizations that empower their teams' sense of satisfaction, joy, and basic wellbeing leverage that basic human need (to feel worthy) to their advantage. Such organizations simply perform better than those that don't.

This isn't a religious perspective – church organizations are subject to the same basic human needs as business enterprises! Atheists aren't exempt from the humanity we all share and the powerful way that spiritual attributes, such as appreciation, can motivate people. This is a big part of why we have adopted the word "spiritual" as a term for all the intangible attributes that make a real difference in organizations. To be very clear, it's true that some of the language we must use to discuss such things is common to religions and belief systems of all kinds, but our objective here is mutual understanding. This conversation will take extra care to clearly define what is meant by terms such as "appreciation" and "joy" in the context of how practicing them in an organization makes that organization more successful.

Therefore, when we speak of "spiritual growth," we understand that many of us will evaluate that term from our own experience and background, and that each of us will have a distinct and personal energy around that term. It's equally true that there's much about the process of change in organizations that's anything but sublime, but if you recognize that a larger purpose is served in organizational growth or change, and take a peek at some of the intangible aspects of the process, you can start to understand why spirituality in organizations matters. In fact, spirituality is vital to an organization's sustainability, and it always has been.

WHY THIS BOOK?

When I worked for IBM in the mid 1980s, the organization was in the throes of change. The company was about to experience its first layoffs. Ever. Something about IBM's fundamental culture was changing in ways that no one could accurately describe. For example, even though I got some strange looks, I was able to get away with wearing modern double-breasted suits instead of the more traditional Brooks Brothers three-button or less-traditional-but-acceptable Armani designs. Career managers told me stories of how, only a few years before, a C-level executive could wear a new style of rep tie on Monday, and by Wednesday, everyone on his team would be wearing the same tie.

I graduated from the famous IBM marketing school, but it disappointed the musician in me that we weren't taught the IBM song.[2] Yes: Back in the day, IBM and a number of other companies with similar industrial histories had company anthems, sung regularly like college alma maters, and there are 21st Century examples as well.[3] Like many such songs, those anthems were part of the glue that had held IBM's culture together.

There was no question of IBM's excellence, but the personal computer threatened the core assumptions IBM had practiced successfully for many years. Those core assumptions included things like IBM's legendary market domination, the "right" products, and "right" the kind of talent to achieve and retain market share. Within a few short years, all those assumptions had to change, and they had to change within an organization whose core identity had already begun to erode. The people who would remain at IBM would be very different from its traditional employees up to that point. To survive the change, IBM would be challenged all the way to its core values – its spiritual values, if you will – and would be required to re-invent itself around those values to meet a marketplace exploding with demand for personal computing resources.

IBM's challenge – to re-invent itself around its core values – is a macro example of organizational spiritual growth. Certainly IBM came up with new products and services, re-tooled its capabilities to produce and deliver them, re-structured its marketing organization to work successfully with new kinds of customers, and re-positioned its brand to the world, but it had to do those things within a culture of extreme conformity. Today we might call such a culture "replicable" instead of "authoritarian." Fortunately for IBM, the expectations embodied in its cultural history were set so high that to join and work within that culture was prized as one of the very best careers anyone might achieve. This meant that IBM also enjoyed a long history of superior leaders and employees, so the expectation of conformity to the IBM culture was simply a "given" – part of the price we workers paid for the honor of working there.

There was an IBM employee handbook, of course. As I recall, it was boring reading. Noticeably absent from it was any discussion of how to actually practice the IBM culture. Either you fit in or not; no handbook was going to offer you clues. Like me, if you realized that your true color wasn't IBM blue, you simply offered up your resignation.

Leaving IBM was, in that way, a bit like leaving a church. My core beliefs didn't mesh with the IBM culture, so I left. Nothing wrong with either set of beliefs: I was entrepreneurial and IBM at that time wasn't, so our match wasn't sustainable, and I was the one expected to make the change (fit in or leave). I learned something about myself that I would not have clarified otherwise – one might call this "spiritual growth" – and IBM went on with its process of discovering how to play well in the new world of the Personal Computer and Internet.

The IBM cultural handbook that might have saved me a couple years' professional self-discovery didn't exist back then. Instead, that handbook was written inside every IBMer, and if you could emulate your leaders well you could survive and thrive. Military chain of command is a lot like that: military leaders imbue recruits with the value system of their organization right from the start, and the expectations for conformity to those values are at the core of everything the military does, from waking up in the morning to going to sleep at night. Such cultures work really well when everyone participates, whether in the armed forces or at IBM.

What if IBM had had such a handbook? From the interview process to marketing school I had a number of opportunities to discover exactly how blue I could be, and I might have saved myself some discomfort by learning about my fit sooner rather than later, but the intrinsic attributes of an IBMer just weren't things anyone could have written down! The organization embodied its own best practices and, while many of us read Steven Covey's "7 Basic Habits of Highly Successful People" and Peters' and Waterman's "In Search of Excellence," no one actually discussed the *practice* of IBM's core values in real life everyday situations: either you had it or you didn't.

Fortunately for organizations, business research and analysis has been extended into the territory of the collective attributes of organizational success and fulfillment. Jim Collins' excellent work in the "Good to Great" series is just one recent example of the interest the business community now takes in going beyond merely replicable processes and procedures to the intangible advantages many organizations have discovered that help them soar into excellence.

Those intangibles have become so common among successful organizations that they deserve a generic handbook of their own, useful to any organization of any size. There are obviously parallels between the practice of personal growth and the practice of organizational growth, so it seems reasonable that a guide for beneficial personal practice as it scales up to organizational practice is a worthwhile endeavor. Now is an excellent time to document the attributes of true organizational success for what they are: not materialistic markers or billionaire portfolios, which are just one set of possible success symptoms, but authentic practices of spirituality in real life.

Simply put, the evidence shows that the practice of spirituality works, and organizations that embrace spiritual practices are the ones doing the most good in the world today, both as sustainable engines in their enterprises and as fuel for their team members' wellbeing and livelihood. The spiritual practices that make that possible are ones many more of us could learn and use – a practice as simple as a conscious choice.

Distress, Depression, and Anxiety

Wouldn't you rather practice enthusiasm, joy, and excitement? Did you know that there's a choice, even on the job? The contrast between distress and enthusiasm is huge, as it is between depression and joy or anxiety and excitement. An organization can be lit up with the positive practices, or darkened with the negative ones. We all understand that contrast is a natural part of our universe; from sub-atomic particles to the movement of galaxies, vibration is the over-arching theme of our existence. Lights on; lights off. Happy; sad. Nuclear energy. The contrast is everywhere.

Our human trend toward the feelings we don't want is getting harder to resist, isn't it? The more we honestly examine our human condition, the less apparent cause we have to be happy about it. We have a human tendency to rubberneck drama – provided it's not happening to us – and we feel safe enough to watch it from a distance. Trouble is, our practice of this tendency brings the drama closer. Drama used to live in the newspaper, which we could choose to read or not. Then television made the "read or not" choice a bit more convenient and simultaneously more intriguing. Social media has its uses, but what if one of them is influencing large numbers of people to believe things that aren't true? Drama – and the feelings that go along with it – can be habit-forming, even addictive; this is not a good thing for the human organism.

Millions of people have always united around a crisis of one kind or another, sometimes for a good purpose and sometimes simply to commiserate. Misery has always loved company, it's said, and the World Health Organization agrees. WHO has measured the spread of "unipolar depressive disorders" and the trend is not good: our global village is more distressed, depressed, and anxious now than at any time in measurable history,[4] and things haven't improved.

It's easy to be sucked into the vortex of unipolar depressive disorders, but there are organizations whose work exists outside the drama vortex. In fact, many organizations do what they do *because* of that vortex, especially ones that serve disadvantaged people, and some of them are for-profit, capitalist corporations instead of tax-advantaged not-for-profits! Here's a quote from one such company's website which proves that even capitalists can do the right thing:

> "sammysoap is a job creation machine for adults with intellectual disabilities *disguised* as the world's best soap company. We are not a not-for-profit, on purpose. We manage to the strengths of our employees to make the best soap around. We exist in support of human health, a clean planet, and **disability wage equality**."[5]

Would you like to peek into sammysoap's employee handbook? Do you think people who work in that organization are distressed, depressed, and anxious? It's a good guess that sammysoap team members are much less distressed, depressed, and anxious than they could be! Why not give "adults with intellectual disabilities" the opportunity to thrive? Such ideas and the organizations built around them aren't just good or great, they are superior.

Instead of replaying distressing, depressing and anxiety-producing drama, wouldn't you rather spend some time working alongside people who thrive? Nothing wrong with contrast – that's how things work – but one possible reason things seem to be "getting worse" is *not* that there's too much angst! Perhaps it's because we've neglected to do our part to inject anti-angst into our lives? Making soap is hard work, but it's work you will do happily if you have a disability that prevents you from doing any other kind, and it's more self-empowering, self-affirming and probably more lucrative than taking a handout on a street corner or a disability payment from the government. When you see qualities such as joy or happiness combined with useful work there's a good chance you are witness to an organization's spiritual practice.

Suicide

A Nobel laureate in economics recently got curious about suicide in America, so she did some research. Her study found that middle-aged white men who didn't attend college are killing themselves so fast that they are skewing mortality rates for their entire demographic.[6] We have all heard the famously inaccurate "22 per day" suicide rate among American military Veterans (it's actually more like 170 per day). To put those numbers in a more global context, according to World Health Organization:

"Almost 1 million lives are lost yearly due to suicide, which translates to 3000 suicide deaths every day. For every person who completes a suicide, 20 or more may attempt to end his or her life."[7]

To over-simplify, one possible explanation for the increase in suicide rates may be as simple as the explosion of unipolar depressive disorders: if people get to such a hopeless point of distress, depression and anxiety without any kind of relief, why keep living? Even suicide, however, has arguably spiritual aspects, such as when it's done in protest, or as a dignified end of life after a chronic illness. There are, of course, also thrill-seeking adrenalin-pumped "I don't care if it kills me" suicides, and the recently-fashionable "suicide by cop," but for this discussion we will constrain the conversation to what might be called "preventable" suicide – suicides resulting from feelings of hopelessness and extreme lack of meaning in life.

This book is one pathway to help forestall suicide even before the precursor feelings of uncontrollable distress, depression and anxiety set it. Human beings feel such things quite appropriately when faced with crises that trigger them, but chronic helplessness just isn't good for us because it can lead to a place where it's too easy to spin out of control and lose perspective. The best suicide intervention we humans have is one another, and participation in an organization that helps us find and own our individual meaning can be a powerful way to keep the thoughts of suicide at bay, well back of the tendency toward distress, depression, and anxiety. Working alongside others with whom we share meaning, belonging, and passionate purpose helps break the unipolar depressive disorder habit. It also makes forming or reforming such a habit much more difficult. In that environment, suicide can become much less likely.

THE SCOPE OF THIS BOOK

Once we become objectively conscious of the drama – that is, once we can separate the drama from our own need to experience it – we also begin to see the many social ills that can distract us from our productive, passionate work. Homelessness, mental illness, hunger, clean water, war, income inequality, destructive fundamentalism in all its forms – these are only a few of society's troubles. Our conversation here can impact organizations devoted to change in these areas as well as organizations engaged in production of goods or commercial services or entertainment or the arts, or families… just about any team can benefit from an understanding of organizational spiritual practice. Therefore, this book isn't confined to one specific type of organization, but is written in such a way that it can be used by teams as small as a mentor and protégé or as large as an entire enterprise.

This book is also a companion to two novels about social change: "American Scream: A Novel of Hope and Possibilities," and "The Genius Club for Survivors Only, A Novel of Life and Survival in Declining America," both authored by Rob Reider.[8] While fictional, these books echo real life in many ways, and this book may refer back to them from time to time, although no specific knowledge of either novel is necessary to understand and use the information presented here. No spoiler alert required.

Organizational Development

From the smallest grass-roots organization to the largest multi-national corporation, spiritual skills are relevant and necessary. Whether a mature enterprise finds itself in need of dramatic adaptation to changes around it or a brand new humanitarian organization is just finding its footing, there are powerful spiritual practices waiting to be built into the policies, procedures and cultures those teams project to the world. This book will explore examples of the actual results of doing that. It's also an invitation to you and your organization to participate in what may be the largest, focused reinvigoration of the way people work together that the world has yet seen: global spiritual organizational development.

The world certainly needs reinvigorating. It is a difficult thing to participate in solutions to the world's problems. It's time to encourage a careful exploration of how specific spiritual practices in an organization's development plan can supercharge positive performance and smooth the process of change.

No need to reinvent anything. There are already many successful examples of spiritual thinking and action in organizations. As you become adept in the terminology and understand the effects of spiritual practice, you may find that your personal sphere of influence already includes people and teams practicing spiritually. There's nothing especially difficult about building spiritual practices into an organization once teams and team leaders agree to do so together. Spiritual practices can be modeled successfully and are scalable. They can snap into human resource training, augment change and growth plans, and strengthen manager/subordinate interactions. It's actually fun to bring a new spiritual practice into an organization, so barriers to entry are low.

The biggest issue for organizations that want to embrace spirituality in tangible ways is getting over that word: "spiritual." That will be the subject of the next chapter. First, it may help to consider examples of two rather obvious spiritual practices that have been in use in organizations for some time with consistently positive results: motivation and mentoring.

The Spiritual Practice of Motivation

When I was in my third year of high school, my Mom thought it would be a good idea for me to have a business of my own. The business she chose for me was Amway. I don't remember a lot about the experience, but it certainly exposed me to the early days of network marketing. There were some fired-up people in Amway! Attending a large-scale network marketing business meeting was like going to a pep rally. Lots of hoopla and cheering crowds. I was a bit put off by all the rah-rah because it didn't really work for me as a teenager, but there's no denying that it produces results: Amway is the number one "direct sales" company in the world.[9]

Of course, motivation isn't exclusive to network marketing. The practice of inspiring people to achieve is a very old spiritual practice. There are examples in the wisdom literature of every major tradition on Earth: religious, governmental, philosophical, and educational. The practice of motivation can be called "spiritual" because it is about encouraging people to be and do their best. It demands that we look inside ourselves to find and express our best effort, best communication, best compassion, best teamwork. If you have any doubt about the abilities of an expert modern motivator, take a look at the very impressive documentary "I Am Not Your Guru," which explores the ways in which Tony Robbins is able to encourage people to a spiritual practice of their very best selves.[10]

The degree to which anyone can be an effective motivator varies, as does our receptivity to being motivated. If you understand that your response to motivation is widely regarded as a beneficial thing for your organization, and that your individual response comes from within you, you are well on your way to understanding spiritual practice in organizations.

The Spiritual Practice of Mentoring

My volunteer work over the last several years has included working directly with homeless and at-risk people as well as Veterans recovering from substance abuse. Along the way, I have had the privilege to observe many humanitarian organizations at close range, specifically in the "Veterans transition" process. (For clarity, a transitioning Veteran is making a career change: from active-duty military service to civilian employment; often this can involve a geographic relocation, going back to trade school or university, changes in income, and sometimes reckoning with physical disabilities.) Here in San Diego County, California, many of the organizations involved in the transition process belong to a coalition where participants share success stories and methods for the benefit of all. There's general agreement in collaboratives that, if any single method consistently exceeds expected results, it is mentoring.

To a Veteran, a mentor is a battle buddy, life coach, friend, and sometimes a parental figure. A mentor will not get you a job, but a mentor will help prepare you to get one. A mentor can be there for you when others aren't, such as the volunteer mentors who support Veterans in the restorative justice system during court-ordered treatment. A mentor could be a colleague whose purpose is to make certain you fit in and achieve success with your responsibilities. Although a protégé is not necessarily an apprentice, a mentor may advocate for your success and teach you practical, professional or mentoring skills. Being a mentor can be one of the most rewarding experiences in life; it makes me so proud when a mentored Veteran becomes a mentor to someone new!

The implication in mentoring that the protégé will become a mentor in turn is actually an encouragement to best practice. It can seem altruistic, but a consistent mentoring practice builds strength in the individuals that populate the organization. A well-instituted mentoring practice at IBM might have helped me stay with the company for a bit longer, or may have helped me understand more clearly why I wasn't as good a fit as the organization deserved and needed.

Mentors aren't paid for what they do; if they were paid, they would be called "life coaches." The built-in "pass it forward" aspect to mentoring would be difficult to value in any case. For the right person, giving unselfishly with no expectation of payback can in itself be a reward, especially when the protégé achieves independence. Organizations that use internal team members as mentors often retain their workers longer and build more cohesive teams.[11]

What makes mentoring a spiritual practice? Just a few reasons:

- The unselfish "good of all" aspect of organizational mentoring;

- The volunteer mindset required of both mentor and protégé;

- The education passed along;

- The lasting and supportive human bond that can develop between mentor and protégé.

Even though guidelines for mentoring are somewhat loose in order for it to work, and expectations vary widely from case to case, mentoring is unusually successful. People who mentor seem to share the desire to "do something good" along with – or for – someone else, just for the sheer pleasure of doing it. Yes, it's possible to fail as a mentor, but a shared willingness to both give and receive makes success much more common. Good mentoring may be the most equitable exchange we humans have, and, although there's no way to value it in money, both mentor and protégé often feel equally rewarded by the experience.

We will explore mentoring more fully when we consider relationships later on in this book because it may in fact be the quintessential spiritual practice for organizations. First, let's really explore what we mean by the word "spiritual" and agree on a common language we can use throughout this book.

CHAPTER TWO

TERMINOLOGY

It helps to have a common set of terms to talk about intangible stuff like spirituality. You've already seen words like "love" and "appreciation." As you become more aware of the practice of appreciation you might also begin to recognize some of its close cousins, such as kindness, compassion, humor, and empathy. An effective mentor <u>must</u> practice these kinds of authentic human attributes. This helps explain why mentoring is a spiritual practice in some degree. Best-of-class educators can also be adroit spiritual practitioners, adept at offering students new and difficult information as well as encouragement and intellectual or humorous sparring to expedite the learning and discovery process.

To make it easy to recognize a practice of spirituality, we'll just **boldface** the spiritual terms from this point forward. You'll still have to think about whether or not any particular spiritual term is a "best" practice, which is the point of the book. "The spiritual practice of **appreciation**" or just "**appreciation**," where the boldfaced word could be interchanged with other practical words, such as **respect,**

praise, or **empathy,** indicates a spiritual skill to practice and use frequently.

WHY IT'S IMPORTANT TO GET THE LANGUAGE RIGHT

Spirituality is a naturally slippery subject, so it's vital to be as specific as possible. Here's a mental tune-up that may help: Do you see how love is merely an intangible feeling until it becomes action? And, that **loving** generally involves acts that are pleasant? "Loving" is practice of the feeling of love; "loving" is a feeling turned into action. Make sense?

So, if we discuss **appreciation** – the act of **being appreciative** or **showing appreciation** to someone else – we are discussing a practice or habit that doesn't have an obviously measureable effect. **Loving** and **appreciation** are qualities of action and difficult to quantify. We understand that the way we act toward someone else is a qualitative impression rather than a quantitative measurement. Ways of acting that produce "good" impressions and/or results are the ones we consider here as "spiritual best practices." For example, to habitually say "thank you" is a spiritual practice of **appreciation**.

It can be hard to know how much **appreciation** is enough, but isn't it obvious that withholding **appreciation** has a different effect than giving it?

With terms, especially spiritual ones, the language we choose is often the difference between a best practice and one that's not so good. For example, **disrespect, condemnation,** or **apathy,** which are, for the purposes of our discussion here, most definitely not best practices, are in fact the kinds of spiritual practices we hope to disrupt and replace with better ones. We will investigate these opposite practices later in this book because they are often a clue to what the "best" practice might be.

A final example of why clarity of terms is essential for this discussion is the important difference between **ethics** and **morality**, or as some like to call it, values. For this book, we use the term **ethics** to refer to universally acceptable best practices, whether spiritual or not, such as "do not kill." **Morality** or values, in contrast, refer to practices that are appropriate for the situation, such as the wartime requirement to kill enemy combatants. **Ethics**, therefore, are the guideposts of "discovery and realization of our spirit, that is, our essential selves," while **morality** or values, which some rightly call "situational ethics," is more concerned with the acceptable policies and procedures that it takes to get the job done in the present moment.

Wouldn't it be nice if the relativism of **morality** and values could give way to the universality of **ethics**? This book is an attempt to encourage organizations to do more of that, so it's anchored in **ethics** while it also promotes a best-practice value system, that is, **morality**.

CULTURE AND THE ORGANIZATIONAL CHART

When human beings with common interests and objectives work closely together in groups or teams, they share an inter-connected energy. We commonly refer to this inter-connected energy as the "culture" of an organization. Within a culture, there's a need for shared vision, decision, and leadership, accomplishment of the work, and some kind of reward system for the makers, visionaries, and leaders.

Within the structure of the organization, whether you are a visionary C-level executive, a manager leading a team or project, or a task-based front-line maker cranking out a product or service, you can practice spirituality. Your organization may have different terms for the various positions on the organizational chart; we leave the translation of them up to you. In fairness, this discussion will steer around over-reliance on any particular level of organizational leadership in favor of a broader, culture-based perspective.

Development of a consistent spiritual practice – often called "aligning with the culture" in organizations – has always been a part of success, both on the job where talent and diligence are exchanged for treasure, and in one's personal life where discovering and realizing one's spirit – one's essential self – is essential for an individual to thrive. The remarkable thing is that, as organizations embrace the benefits of spiritual practice, the old "corporate" culture can become a fertile place for nurturing the discovery of our individual spirit.

The traditional hierarchical org chart still exists of course, as well as a whole variety of hybrid structures that serve the particular requirements of the underlying culture. This evolution in itself could be the spiritual practice of an organization discovering new ways to support its essential mission. No single way is any more spiritual than any other; the important things to understand are:

A. Spiritual practice can work both inside and outside of the org chart, individually and collectively;

and:

B. Organizations that model excellent results often practice spiritually, even though they might not refer to that practice using spiritual terms.

Whatever structure your organization may have, it is possible to apply spiritual practices within it, whether top-down or bottom-up. Your organization's "mission statement" is a great example of a top-down spiritual practice. The culture of your team or working group may include bottom-up spiritual practices, from team-building exercises to the small courtesies you offer one another that make getting the job done just a bit easier. The "how to" of such things comes in more detail later in this book. The next section will give you some ideas to spark creative examination of the language your organization speaks around spiritual practice.

HOW TO TRANSFORM EXISTING LANGUAGE INTO SPIRITUAL LANGUAGE

Why is it necessary to understand words like "**appreciation**" or "**mentoring**" as some kind of spiritual term? To answer that question, let's refer back to the quantitative and qualitative nature of this discussion.

Organizations generally measure their mission in quantitative terms: how many widgets we made, how many people we served. Over time, effective organizations get better and better at doing those things, so they begin to differentiate themselves by creatively integrating intangibles into their widgets or services.

For example, when Southwest Airlines originated the "cattle call" boarding process, they specifically used **humor** to engage passengers and elicit cooperation. It worked so well that Southwest was able to turn a plane from arrival to departure faster than their competitors, and therefore serve more passengers and grow their organization into an enjoyable model of low-cost air travel. For a while, Southwest had a comedy track running as its music on hold, and Southwest flight crews' comedic departure safety reviews were the envy of the industry. People *wanted* to be on hold, queue up to board their crowded flights, and couldn't wait to hear the latest oxygen mask shtick. Southwest Airlines tapped into an essential spiritual practice (qualitative) to surpass their competition and turn in remarkable results (quantitative).

To get the results they did, was it necessary for Southwest to identify **humor** as a spiritual practice? Of course not. But it was a masterstroke, since in commercial airline organizations back then, there weren't too many ways to attract and keep the average passenger. In a similar way, **humor,** always the vehicle for political satire, has now become a much-less-painful and much more palatable way to deliver the news, if the success of "Saturday Night Live Weekend Update" and "The Daily Show" are any indication. What a brilliant way for bad news to seem not so bad, and for an airline to bring passengers on board, both literally and figuratively. If you traveled by air in those days, it's a good bet you have a memorable and humorous story or two to tell.

Air travel and broadcast news aren't the only industries that have reached a stalemate in the "more for less" chess game. The social services industry has always done more with less, and the demands for universal health insurance coverage are pushing the limits of what can be done at all. Angst-laden industries like these are huge opportunities for spiritual best practice.

As we will see in the next chapters, leading organizations embrace spiritual practices for what they are: essential drivers of culture, employee engagement, and success. There's an unstoppable trend behind the demise of old euphemisms like "on-boarding," "thought leadership," "make it happen," "best of breed," change management," "take ownership" and "pain point." To make the transformation to spiritual language is easy...and timelessly cliché-free. Many of the terms are already in common use and only require clarification of purpose. By way of example, see if you can catch the spiritual best practice at work in just a few of the headlines and bullet points from articles collected while researching this book.

Bullet point headers from the gyro/FORTUNE Knowledge Group study "Beyond the Brand:"[12]

• Stand for something

• Dial up the soul of your business

- Live by your principles

Ten or even twenty years ago, those bullets might have read this way:

- Mission First

- What are we fighting for?

- Rules to live by

Do you see how the older language has evolved to meet the current demand for things like "soul" and "principles" instead of conflict and rules?

From The Boston Globe, November 10, 2015: "The Surprising Power of Being Nice to Your Employees."[13]

Being nice to your employees? When was that ever a recognized mark of excellence or longevity in business... until now?

From Entrepreneur Magazine, September 30, 2015: "7 Guidelines for Entrepreneurs to Do the Right Thing, Whatever that Means."[14]

Imagine: doing the "right thing" versus doing what's best for the organization? Clearly, the shift has been in favor of organizations whose "right thing" is best for the organization *and* those it serves.

And finally, an in-depth scholarly paper on spiritual development and military readiness written for the United States Army (previously cited above), which includes an extensive discussion of the spiritual practice of **resilience**:

"Building Spiritual Fitness in the Army – An Innovative Approach to a Vital Aspect of Human Development."[15]

The Army paper takes the most direct approach to spiritual terms, but there's nothing wrong with characterizing the practices of standing for something, dialing up the soul of your business, living by your principles, being nice, or doing the right thing for what they are: essential – perhaps vital – aspects of human development and transformation. Therefore, in this book, we describe them that way: spiritual best practices at work in organizations.

We've seen some examples of spiritual best practices in culture and principles, so let's extend that discussion to organizational brand, and bravely bust apart the taboos around relationships, politics and economics.

CHAPTER THREE

SPIRITUAL BEST PRACTICES

What are some spiritual best practices at work in organizations? There are many, of course, so we will confine our discussion to just six areas, and identify some key practices at work in each one, to give you a start in thinking about how to incorporate these practices into your organization. The areas we will consider as examples are:

- Culture

- Principles

- Brand

- Relationships

- Politics

- Economics

CULTURE

How does it feel to work for a particular organization? Does working there align with who you really are (**authentic**), or does it take effort to be someone you're really not when you show up to work (**fake**)? Do you "fit" the work environment well, or struggle, the way I did at IBM? Culture is that intangible, qualitative presence or energy that surrounds you and everyone on your team as you work together. It's not tied down to perks such as the team retreat or a physical place like a farm-to-table cafeteria. Distributed, work-from-home teams can have very pronounced cultures, too.

What spiritual practices support culture? **Empathy**, **respect**, **appreciation**, **humor**, and **kindness** are a few. Dial those practices down and the resulting culture will be much different from the culture of an organization that practices them consistently. The individual practice of culture has always been important within an organization, but – funny thing! – studies show that organizations themselves prefer to work with other strong-culture organizations![16] Organizations are learning that there's a choice: why work with the turkeys when you can soar with the eagles?

PRINCIPLES

What does your organization stand for? Is there a palpable connection between its mission and its day-to-day? Does everyone share a common understanding of the purpose of the work? Is there a shared commitment to "doing the right thing?" If so, there's a good chance spiritual practices such as **integrity, consistency, vision, excellence,** and **discretion** are in active use. Organizations that don't value their principles are generally also deficient in those practices.

There's a big difference here between organizations that are unethical and organizations that are just unprincipled. A fast-growing dynamic organization may need time to nurture some healthy principles, while an unethical organization's principles may be well established in practice. For example, even though it was an unethical and illegal Ponzi scheme, one could argue that Bernie Madoff[17] ran an organization of **integrity, consistency, vision, excellence** and **discretion.**

Taken together, an organization's culture and principles ought to be consistent and aligned to achieve best practice. What's the point of practicing **integrity, consistency, vision, excellence** and **discretion** when **empathy, respect, appreciation, humor,** and **kindness** are absent? And, unless culture and principles are aligned, how can an organization ever sustain itself or its brand?

BRAND

An organization's outward-facing image is its brand. A successful brand connects the culture and principles of the organization that created it with the culture and principles of those who want its products or services. Service organizations such as Red Cross, United Way, or Habitat for Humanity are eponymous successful brands, as are the product brands Band-Aid, Kleenex and WD-40.

Celebrities, artists and musicians, whose name is their brand, offer a wide variety of additional examples.

What are some of the spiritual practices of "brand?"

Possibly the biggest brand-impacting spiritual practice is **authenticity**. Organizations that can't or don't practice **authenticity** when branding their product or service are quickly dissed and exposed. In relationships, human beings share a desire for the authentic, and successful organizations capitalize on that shared desire. To offer the most authentic product or service demands a practice that connects that offering with the culture and principles behind it.

One thought-provoking example of the spiritual practice of **authenticity** is Donald Trump. A refreshing aspect of Trump's brand is its **authenticity**, which many voters found attractive in the 2016 US election. "You get what you pay for" is another practice of **authenticity**, and regardless of how despicable the man Donald Trump may be, his branding is consistent with who he is. There's no doubt that America will get what it paid for, whether or not we individually voted for the man. Still, like Bernie Madoff, Donald Trump illustrates how spiritual best practices, when used without ethics, can potentially go very wrong.

Another intriguing spiritual practice of "brand" is **loyalty**. Imagine Coke or Pepsi tampering with the recipe! Yes: it's happened, and loyal customers felt betrayed. Was it **disloyal** to try something new? You decide: which spiritual practice is best?

If you enjoy wearing logo shoes or clothing, or driving a particular luxury automobile, or prefer using one manufacturer's mobile device instead of another, you'll understand something else about **loyalty** and its close cousins **honor** and **humility**. These spiritual best practices relate closely to brand, and successful organizations decide precisely how to offer their products or services so that their brand is consistent with best spiritual practice. High-end luxury brands and cost-conscious value brands intentionally appeal to a consumers' or clients' **honor** or **humility** as a direct, intentional consequence of the organization's underlying spiritual practice of **honor** or **humility**. Genuine Louis Vuitton luggage doesn't have to fool anyone, but the cheap knock-off, produced by an organization with a much different appreciation for – and practice of – culture and brand, results from a much different practice of **honor** and **humility**.

To explore this a bit further, let's investigate **honor**. Years ago, I read an interview with a craftsman whose day job was machining and assembling vertical vanes for the grille of a particular model of Rolls Royce automobile. The man was so proud of his talents, and he treated his position as the **honor** it was to be chosen for the job. He had become one of the very few craftsmen ever to hold that position, and he performed it as his spiritual practice of the Rolls Royce brand: every Roller that craftsman touched was a testament to the **honor** with which he performed his job.

Humility holds a special place for me personally in the practice of brand. Because I do quite a bit of volunteer work with homeless people, I recognize that part of my personal brand demands that I treat all people with

equity, even those people society has literally kicked to the curb. I have been humbled to watch people both permanently rise above homelessness as well as continually choose to be homeless. Practicing **humility** is a big part of my personal brand – I can't do my work without practicing **humility**.

Tax-advantaged organizations understand **humility** practically from the first day they open their doors. To be successful as a not-for-profit or social benefit corporation demands a practice of **humility**, whether asking donors for funds or providing services to clients. This is not to say that tax-advantaged organizations are in any way excluded from the spiritual practice of **abundance**! Of course, a culture with well-grounded principles produces a much different brand than one without, and even though both kinds can encourage **loyalty**, their practices of **authenticity** may differ greatly.

Are you beginning to get a sense of the interconnected nature of spiritual practice in organizations with respect to their outward-facing brand? Now, to get to the heart of what fuels an organization, let's examine spiritual practice at the most basic level: one-to-one relationships.

RELATIONSHIPS

It's a loaded term, but if we think of relationships in the broadest possible way, the spiritual practices become clear. What spiritual practices are common to any relationship, from acquaintance to client to customer to friend to boss to mentor to teammate? We could start with the very same ones that sustain culture: **empathy, respect, appreciation, humor,** and **kindness,** then add **authenticity** and **integrity. Humility** can be a useful spiritual practice in relationships. Depending on the depth of the relationship, **loyalty** is also a best practice. **Courage** is a best spiritual practice when your side of the relationship becomes difficult.

Are any of those spiritual best practices alive and well in your relationships? If they predominate, chances are good that your relationships are also mostly good. If you notice your relationships are missing **empathy,** full of **disrespect,** or scoring very low on **appreciation, humor** and **kindness,** you are missing the satisfaction of best spiritual practice. If your work environment mirrors your personal one, it's time to make some changes! Do you see the **contrast** between active spiritual best practices and their absence?

Discourse about relationships grew roots long before the "harm no one" tenant of ancient spiritual practice. Human relationships are a much wider subject than we can explore fully in this simple book, but the relevant point is that our relationships are the building blocks to how an organization gets stuff done.

To build on this discussion, it may be useful to explore our relationship to topics that are somewhat removed from the work of an organization: politics and economics.

POLITICS

For this part of the discussion, if you think of "politics" on the national scale, not a limited intra-office or inter-organizational one, it will help tune up your objectivity for when we consider the specific politics in your office or organization in the chapter on Implementation.

Don't politics and spiritual best practices seem at odds most of the time? Character assassination and the cheap vilification of one's political opponent(s) are not talents needed to govern effectively, especially when the people "on the other side of the aisle" participate in the same government. In America and other countries, the "permanent campaign" and the political news cycle can eclipse the progress made by politicians actually doing the job they promised to do. So, how can spiritual best practices have a real role in today's politics?

You may intrinsically know something about how spiritual best practices work in organizations where teams share a common goal. How can these same spiritual best practices work in the political realm, where part of the process is that co-workers overheat in opposition to each other? We need to take a close look at how the sometimes-extreme **contrast** in politics animates our viewpoints, and how to turn that energy toward a productive objective.

As before, let's begin with some of the terms. These words may be familiar but perhaps you haven't yet noticed them as spiritual practices. Here are just a few of the "best" ones alongside the relevant "less-than-best" practice terms:

- **dialogue**, instead of **argument** or **debate**, which have acquired an unjustly negative connotation;

- **compromise**, versus **dispute**, **dissent**, or **stonewall;**

- **altruistic**, not **egotistic** or **mean;**

- **cooperative** or **collaborative**, instead of **exploitive** or **abusive**;

- **ethical** versus **unethical**.

Can you see how the terms themselves seem to evoke two different kinds of feelings...some would say energies? The positive or negative connotation of the terms themselves is a big clue to whether or not they are a "best" practice: in general, a positive connotation lines up behind a best spiritual practice. For example, **criticism** used to be a constructive term, and while "critical thinking" retains some of that "best" intent, "critics" don't wear the same mantle of respect that they used to, such that many of them are now called "pundits."

Politics is a great playground for recognizing both what works as a best spiritual practice and what does not, perhaps because the actual work politicians accomplish, when it happens, gets so much attention, both positive and negative. The mega-**contrast** in politics is a key to identifying best spiritual practices. For example, America celebrated wildly when the Affordable Care Act became law, and the handwringing about its repeal or transformation is just as noisy: both circumstances offer excellent opportunities to observe **contrast** in action.

We see plenty of speechifying and demagoguery in politics, but very little actual lawmaking makes the news. Even so, we believe that somewhere inside the core of every politician is something intensely motivational – some impetus to want to make a difference. Yes, it's true that while some politicians run for office for the ego boost or the money, it's equally true that politicians share a desire to do the right thing, whatever they believe that might be. It may seem like a stretch, but this assumption helps us connect to character traits worthy of practice as spiritual bests, like these:[A]

- **honor;**

- **dignity;**

- **respect;**

- **compassion;**

- **fairness;**

- **vision;**

- **integrity;**

- **consistency.**

We can only hope that "best" character traits animate the politicians we elect! It's unfortunate that when politicians pay homage to a best spiritual practice like

---

A   This is NOT an exhaustive list!

compassion, compassionate action doesn't always follow their words. Perhaps, just like most people, some politicians are simply more deficient than others, and it's just as likely that some politicians use spiritual practices unethically. If nothing else, this illustrates an important truism about spiritual practice (hat tip to the French Revolution and Spider-Man's Uncle Ben, among others):

> *Spiritual best practices have great power, and with great power comes great responsibility.*

Don't we elect powerful leaders with the presumption that they will act responsibly? Even miscreants can be elected – elected office seems to attract more and more electable but despicable people – but don't voters believe deeply that their candidate *will* do the right thing? There's equally great passion behind the animus of conservatives, liberals, libertarians, and statists alike, so how can we know in advance of our vote whether any candidate will be "best?" In truth, we can't. But, if we are aware of the **contrast** between best spiritual practices and other, not-so-good spiritual practices, participation in the election process (and **acceptance** of the results!) can get easier and less frustrating.

As hard as it is to consistently practice best character traits – some might say it's simply unrealistic – we don't need a perfect performance, just one that's better. Remember the reason for this book? Spiritual best practices distinguish people and organizations that practice them as best in class, best of breed, best performers, best places to work, best to do business with. Combine the spiritual best practices with the tasks of any given enterprise and that enterprise will soar...yes, even in politics.

It's not difficult to recall extremely popular politicians who also practiced spiritual best. Here are two enormous examples, one from each side of the judgment history makes about such people.

A popular, charismatic, and visionary politician restored Germany to power after World War I. Hitler was the darling of much of the world in the early 1930s, and assumed more and more power with the assent and cooperation of the German people who justifiably loved him. Other popular, charismatic and visionary politicians had to stop the genocide Hitler eventually inflicted on Germans and the megalomania he thrust on Europe. History makes no excuse for Hitler, but, even though he is largely viewed with utter disdain, it cannot be said that he was deficient in **vision** and **integrity;** he continued a single focus right through to his own dogged demise. Hitler's story is a clear indication that spiritual best practices were significantly compromised by the morality at work in his case.

President Obama's rise to power also illustrates how a politician can capture the imagination of a nation. In his case, hoped-for, vast worldwide change didn't follow directly from his huge popularity; as beloved as Obama was in America, America became much less beloved on the world stage during Obama's tenure, and for much different reasons than those which heaped wrath on Germany in the 1930s and 1940s. Of all his spiritual best practices,

Obama's **vision, compassion** and **integrity** seem to have most guided his governance, even though those best practices may have not had the positive impact on the world that Obama wanted. History will doubtless reflect on his Presidency and re-write his story many times, so a common understanding and appreciation of the eight years Obama spent leading the free world may take decades to coalesce, but this takes nothing away from the character attributes that attracted voters to him in the first place. Those character attributes may be the best way to evaluate spiritual best practices in politics.

Exercise **vision** and **integrity** without **dignity** or **respect** and you get a Hitler redux. Conversely, even when **vision, integrity, dignity,** and **respect** are obviously in play, there's no guarantee that they can change the world – at least on the political stage!

Frustrated? Yeah. Imagine how Obama must have felt. Or any world leader. Or anyone serving on a volunteer board. Or corporate board. Are you getting the picture? **Frustration** is part of it. You can use that.

Do you understand that **contrast** and **frustration** are part of the political process, but not the whole of it? Politics without **honor, dignity, respect, compassion, fairness, vision, integrity, consistency,** and other spiritual best practices becomes a morass, a swamp, gridlock, and (insert your favorite derogatory term here).

At its heart, politics is the skillful manipulation of discourse – the process of advocating a particular point of view in conversation with those advocating for a contrasting one. When that conversation devolves into a shouting match the political process can seem like a kindergarten sandbox brawl. Such things fascinate a drama- and scandal-hungry public, but they don't serve the cause of good governance. Unfortunately, the public pays the price when politics aren't practiced skillfully and good governance is sacrificed for the angst that fuels the news cycle.

We like to think that national leaders exercise their power responsibly. Fortunately, the process of political discourse helps to put a brake on a politician's ability to exercise power. Still, even in representative democracies, "executive orders" – government by fiat – are one way that an elected leader can mandate change. Fortunately, in America, there are checks and balances even on Presidential executive orders. America's recent fascination with executive orders has forced a necessary sort of political discourse on the rest of us. How we respond to that opportunity – to evaluate the wisdom of our leaders' decisions – gives each of us a choice of which spiritual practices to employ.

How do you respond to ideas that oppose your core beliefs? It is possible to engage in **dialogue** and expect forward-moving or even forward-focused results? Can politics retain an ability to be constructively **deliberative** without also being destructive? Can *you*?

National politics begins at a personal level. That is, what we practice in our personal day-to-day tends to scale up in our choices of relationship, employment, leadership (political or otherwise), and economy. Our passionate beliefs underlie our practices, and this book isn't about altering or even questioning those beliefs. In this section, we are most interested in how to engage spiritual best practices around those beliefs and passions in a way that skillfully advances ideas.

To do that there's no requirement that we sell out on our beliefs or passions; that would be the opposite of the spiritual best practice of **integrity**. In fact, spiritual best practices in politics demand that we become skilled at the arts of **dialogue** and persuasion as well as understanding and **compassion**. Regardless of how committed we are to one point of view, there's simply no way to advance that point of view successfully and sustainably without **cooperation**, and extending **dignity** to those whose point of view is different from ours is the first step. One doesn't even have to engage in a discussion to research and evaluate an opposite point of view, but it takes a degree of **humility** to objectively understand ideas that seem so far outside one's familiar wheelhouse. It takes some effort to do this.

There are easier ways, including coercion and **manipulation**. Coercion – a threat to one's treasure, talent or time – is not a spiritual practice; **manipulation**, which involves the aspect of subtle choice, is a spiritual practice, although it may not always be a "best" one. I prefer the **manipulation** of reality in a good science fiction movie, for example, to the **coercion** of a tax audit. In politics, you might be able to get me to see and accept your point of view by **manipulation**, but it will be very difficult to accept your point of view if you coerce my vote with threats or empty promises. *How* you present your passionate beliefs matters; take the easy way and perhaps win the day, or engage best spiritual practices in the dialogue for a better shot at a collaborative, sustainable outcome.

An individual spiritual best practice of **acceptance** is key in the realm of politics. It takes **courage** to clearly see and accept what is, and there can be no way forward without clear **consensus** about the underlying facts and issues. To build that foundation demands leadership with **vision** for a better tomorrow, **respect** and **honor** for many different points of view, and mutual **dignity** between the individuals engaged in the process, since the mutual political objective is, we hope, to continue the conversation until we achieve acceptable agreement. Whether we practice this in relationships or politics makes no difference; it's still a best spiritual practice with predictable results. Ignore the practice and the results will reflect that ignorance.

This is not to say that spiritual best practice is easy in the arena of **compromise** and **disagreement** (the opposite of **agreement** – both spiritual practices by the way)! If it were easy, we wouldn't need a sort of handbook of Spiritual Best Practices for Organizations.

As a final point in this section, let's return to the notion of **contrast** to help sort things out.

Political debate starts with **disagreement**: two or more contrasting points of view. Through **dialogue** the various options are explained, understood, questioned, debated, disparaged, supported, and eventually voted upon. Often, there are big differences – big **contrast** – between the options. As participants in this process, we bring our passionate beliefs to the conversation and advocate strongly for them, just as our colleagues advocate for their differing passionate beliefs. In this example, let us assume that, because we are all skilled communicators with a gift for understanding our colleagues' points of view, we reach some kind of consensus and agree to take a vote. Unfortunately, after hearing all the arguments and weighing all the options, we are still unclear about the best way to move forward. What to do?

Instead of voting for the options with the loudest support (sadly, much of what passes for "best" these days is misunderstood to be what's loudest), we decide to think back through the spiritual best practices suggested in this book and make an evaluation based on them. The decision process for best options might look like this:

1. Options that are obviously **uncompassionate**, **exploitive** (or immoral and unethical) don't make the short list, because these spiritual practices aren't "best" for the organization and aren't best for the individuals in it;

2. Options that sacrifice **dignity** or **respect** are off the short list, too, for the same reasons;

3. Options that embody **honor** and **appreciation** are worthy of consideration because these spiritual best practices have a proven successful track record, but not if the cost is **dishonor** in some other way;

4. Finally, if the deliberative process must result in winners and losers and there is no other way forward, are there "good enough for now"

> options that are spiritual best practices *and* have
> the potential for re-evaluation at a future date?

(If you are reading this closely and recognize a greatly over-simplified version of how America's Affordable Care Act became law, as well as the subsequent party-lines debate about modifying it, kudos to you!)

In this example, **contrast** functions as a sort of radar: which options are **compassionate** and which are not; which options are **exploitive** and which are not. Clearly, this is an imperfect example, because the real political world includes powerful forces that work on our elected representatives, often to the detriment of best spiritual practices and the hopes we constituents had back on Election Day. Still, if we can exercise our ability to evaluate how our elected representatives vote and work through the choices they made based on our individual understanding of best spiritual practice, we can be prepared to be more skillful in how we cast our votes on the next election day.

Normally, on the national stage, a political compromise leaves some parties with less than they hoped to achieve. These areas of unresolved **contrast** must be re-visited until they, too, are resolved sustainably. America's history of civil rights, read from the advent of slavery to the present day, offers such a track record of **contrast** followed by **dialogue** and in some cases coercion (the Civil War), in some cases sustainability (The Civil Rights Act) and in some cases **manipulation** (The Defense of Marriage Act).

Reduced from the national stage to your organization, the same decision process can apply. The best, most sustainable choices, even when disagreement about them remains, happen through use of best spiritual practices. How do we know? We take a close look at whether or not people are buying in to them, both figuratively and literally.

ECONOMICS

Spiritual best practices…and economics? The exchange of time and talent for treasure is one of the most basic human transactions. Even if you have zero knowledge of economics, you participate in this exchange. We are going to spend some extra time on this example because of its foundational importance to all of us.

The act of putting food on our tables is our most basic economics lesson. Everything we eat makes its journey from farms to our tables with many exchanges along the way. That is, the farmer who grows grains as a business exchanges treasure for the seeds, land, equipment, supplies, and talent that result in a crop. The crop itself is exchanged for treasure, delivered for processing (in yet another exchange of treasure for transportation), and finally processed in ways that (hopefully) delight those of us who consume it. More transportation of the finished edible food takes place in yet another exchange, and we hungry consumers ultimately exchange our treasure for the pleasure of a tasty meal.

This simplified example shows how there are multiple exchanges made in the process of providing food to people. The process can be simpler, such as when a farmer saves some of the harvest to feed the farming family, but there's still one or more exchanges of treasure for goods or talent (treasure for seed, for example). The study of these exchanges is the study of economics.

How does spiritual practice enter into this process?

Appreciation

One of the most powerful – some would say *the* most powerful – spiritual practices is **appreciation**, which is closely related to the **gratitude** many people express either silently or audibly by saying grace before a meal. **Appreciation** is a prime motivator in the workplace.[18] Feeling appreciated, it turns out, turns employees into super-workers. **Appreciation** works well with kids, too. So why don't more of us practice it? Isn't the paycheck enough of a bribe to keep us employed? Not really! Here's what Harvard Business Review said recently about **appreciation:**

> "In the workplace itself, researcher Marcial Losada has found that among high-performing teams, the expression of positive feedback outweighs that of negative feedback by a ratio of 5.6 to 1. By contrast, low-performing teams have a ratio of .36 to 1."[19]

Because the workplace – the organization, the home, the team, the relationship – is the place where our engines of economics work, wouldn't it be best if they worked well? If introducing or reinforcing the spiritual practice of **appreciation** is a guaranteed way to make workplaces work better, wouldn't that be a best practice? If your answers to both questions are an enthusiastic "yes!" you are paying attention, and the research agrees.[20]

You may never do this, but what if you had the time and desire to write a quick note of appreciation to every person or organization in the economic chain between your first bite of breakfast and the raw materials and services that went into it? For a brand name breakfast cereal, your list of contributors could be a long one. If you use a farm-to-table delivery service, it's much simpler: the delivery driver or company that packaged the eggs and brought them to your door; the farmer who raised the chickens and provided the eggs to the delivery service; the hens laying the eggs (!). (This is a practice, remember? You can improve anything by practicing it properly, so why not show those chickens some **appreciation?**)

In economics, every time there's an exchange, there's also an opportunity to practice **appreciation**. It takes some practice just to be aware of those exchanges, but once you begin to notice them, they appear everywhere. For the moment, let's not make a value judgment about them; just think about where those exchanges take place and how you can show **appreciation** when they happen. This could be as simple as giving a co-worker the thumbs-up for a job well done, or saying "thank you" when someone's routine task helps you out, too. Much of what organizations do falls into the banal and boring grind, and even that dull roar has many small exchanges in it – exchanges that deserve as much **appreciation** as the significant and monumental moments organizations love to celebrate. Call it "positive feedback" if you like, but do it! Please! **Appreciation** works just as well in a one-to-one relationship as it does scaled up to the entire enterprise, and it tends to be closely connected to **abundance** rather than **scarcity**.

Scarcity

Under the umbrella of economics, this discussion has many points of departure – too many for a brief book – but the spiritual practice of **scarcity** deserves discussion. There's some necessary groundwork to cover before we address **scarcity** itself.

(If you've noticed that **scarcity** is bold-faced as a spiritual practice, you're paying close attention. Please recall that, for this book, there's an implied judgment that some spiritual practices are "best," which also means that there are spiritual practices, such as **scarcity** or **lack** that aren't "best." **Patience,** please! We will discuss these opposing spiritual practices in more detail later in the book.)

A succinct essay on "common goods" in Wikipedia[21] addresses the roots of **scarcity** head-on, and because of today's poignant issues like income disparity and resource depletion, most of that short essay is reproduced here to illustrate both the background and need for the spiritual practices of **equity** or **fairness**. When we speak of "the tragedy of the commons" we refer to the downside of **scarcity**, and this essay explains why.

> "Common goods are defined in economics as goods which are rivalrous and non-excludable. Thus, they constitute one of the four main types of the most common typology of goods[22] based on the criteria:

- whether the consumption of a good by one person precludes its consumption by another person (**rivalrousness**) [our e mphasis]

- whether it is possible to prevent people (consumers) who have not paid for it from having access to it (**excludability**) [also our emphasis]

"One modern example is climate stability. Another is limited employment in terms of jobs available in an economy, which could be farmed out overseas or populated by cheap migrants. More classic examples of common goods are water and air. Water and air can be polluted: water flows can be tapped beyond sustainability, and air is often used in combustion, whether by motor vehicles, smokers, factories, wood fires. Another example of a private **exploitation** [our emphasis] treated as a renewable resource ... have been [sic] trees or timber at critical stages (used for wood and paper), oil (used for plastic, paints, foam, fabric, and often burned to create energy), mined metals (used to create machines, tools, nails, cans, coins), and crops (to become cotton and many kinds of foods). Fish stocks in international waters are also cited often. In this later example (avoiding any issues of the natural rights of the fish)...when fish are withdrawn from the water without any limits being imposed, living stocks of fish are likely to be depleted for any later fishermen. To describe situations in which economic users withdraw resources to secure short-term gains without regard for the long-term consequences, the term '*tragedy of the commons*' was coined.

"Debates about sustainability can be both philosophical and scientific. However, wise use advocates consider common goods which are an exploitable form of a renewable resource, such as fish stocks, grazing land, etc., to be sustainable in the following two cases:

- As long as demand for the goods withdrawn from the common good does not exceed a certain level, future yields are not diminished and the common good as such is being preserved as a 'sustainable' level.

- If access to the common good is regulated at the community level by restricting exploitation to community members and by imposing limits to the quantity of goods being withdrawn from the common good, the tragedy of the commons may be avoided. Common goods which are sustained through an institutional arrangement of this kind are referred to as common-pool resources."

Whether your organization bases its sustainability on **rivalrousness** ("I ate it, so there's none for you!"), **excludability** ("You didn't buy a ticket so you can't come in!"), or **non-excludability** ("Free yoga class every Monday!"), there is *always* expectation of an exchange in the course of your organization's operation. Organizations as small as families and as large as worldwide corporations must conduct exchanges to survive. Organizations that trend toward success generally incorporate spiritual practices in their exchanges – spiritual practices that benefit both the organization and its customers or clients – whether or not they call those practices "spiritual."

Sadly, thanks to growing awareness of the **scarcity** of natural and manufactured resources, income inequality, and general **lack,** society is becoming increasingly aware of the tragedy of the commons, that is, the institutionalized disregard for the long-term consequences of resource use in favor of short-term gains. Many of the inequities we experience are a result of the tragedy of the commons. Still, it is possible to reverse this tragedy, as "wise use advocates" suggest, by 1) limiting demand for a resource so that its future sustainability is maintained or 2) regulating withdrawals of the resource by mutual community agreement. These options institutionalize **scarcity** and don't promote **abundance**.

Equity

The spiritual practice of **equity** addresses the tragedy of the commons. **Equity** is recognition of **fairness** and **impartiality** in the process of exchange. The notions of **equality** and **wise use** are part of the spiritual practice of **equity,** and this alone may explain the biggest difficulty with its practice: How does anyone really know if a particular exchange is equitable or fair? How can it be equitable, for example, that Bernie Madoff was jailed for the crime of running a Ponzi scheme when so many of his investors kept their illegal gains, and so many others lost everything?

The spiritual practice of **equity** is especially demanding on relationships because it implies that both parties in an exchange recognize **fairness** to one another. To do that, one needs to engage the spiritual practices we've discussed under Culture and Principles. Are you beginning to understand that a person or an organization without a strong culture or principles has no real chance at practicing **equity**, and that such a person or organization will instead make exchanges out of **rivalrousness** and **excludability** to the detriment of all other people and organizations? That is the tragedy of the commons…but there's another simpler word for such a shortsighted economic spiritual practice: **greed**.

Clearly, the tragedy of the commons isn't so much of an issue for goods like mobile phone or Internet service… until that service has some technical difficulty that impacts many consumers. Service outages help us remember that even artificially-created resources still require human beings to repair and replace stuff that breaks.

Organizations that provide services also engage in exchange, and therefore must be sensitive to the tragedy of the commons. Services are not exactly "common goods" in that one person's consumption of the service doesn't deplete another's. Instead, "club goods" is the economic term for these services. Examples include: community and social services (non-governmental and public), cable television and Internet, or computer software and applications. Organizations that exchange club goods for treasure can also practice **equity,** and often do so in interesting ways.

A tax-advantaged organization that provides shelter to homeless people exchanges donors' treasure for housing. A church exchanges donors' treasure for religious experience, fellowship, and theological instruction. Internet service and cable television providers exchange treasure for access to the World Wide Web and licensed media content. Software manufacturers, teachers, artists, musicians, writers, and creatives of all kinds exchange treasure for licenses to use their talent and/or their creations. Parents and care-giving professional organizations are also providers of club goods, as are many government agencies.

What tragedy of the commons affects an organization whose main activities are the delivery of club goods (services)? Have you ever spoken with an organization's workers who are attempting to deliver ever more club goods to an ever-increasing demand for them? People doing that can be highly stressed in their jobs (think of your last call to Tech Support or Customer Care!), or insulated by a bureaucracy from being truly effective (think of your last visit to the DMV).

In our early 21st Century, one significant tragedy of the club goods commons is that the human talent available to provide community and social services is not adequately meeting demand. For whatever reason, society expects to receive services from other human beings at a rate that has outstripped the capabilities of the workers who provide them. Health care and unemployment insurance are two very salient examples where **need**, not **greed**, causes a club goods tragedy of the commons. This illustrates the fact that the spiritual practice of **scarcity**, which helps put the brakes on rampant depletion of common-pool resources, is powerless to check the demand for all the club goods to which society increasingly feels it is entitled, such as "free" education and health care, and in some cases housing, disability payments, even telephone service and food.

If a club good (service) is provided to a customer or client without apparent exchange, this means only that the exchange was hidden from view in some way, similar to a not-for-profit that accepts donors' treasure and uses it to provide houses for homeless people. **Scarcity** is still at work (donors' treasure is limited, and the available supply of housing is limited) but this may not be apparent to the homeless person, provided they get shelter.

America's national discourse about health insurance has brought some of these hidden exchanges to light – in fact, the government has misappropriated the entire concept of "exchange" by pretending that its web portals for obtaining health insurance are in any way **equitable**! For example, there are no guarantees that health insurance purchased on a health care "exchange" will be **honored** by health care professionals, who have the freedom to choose whether or not to accept payment from insurance purchased on a government "exchange" (the concept of **excludability**). Is it **equitable** to accept less than adequate treasure in exchange for our talent? In this way, **scarcity** is already at work to put the brakes on health care club goods; even if every

American had "free" health insurance, and could be insulated from the details of the exchange required to make that so, an exchange of treasure for talent must take place, and that exchange must be **equitable** or it cannot be sustained.

As a society, we tend to approach solutions to these issues by applying economic systems. Highly regulated systems like socialism and communism compel common goods and common pool and club good goods allocation through central control. Decentralized economic systems rely on distributed control that anticipates organizations and people will "do the right thing" when it comes to resource allocation. This book doesn't take sides about which economic system is better; we simply want to make the **contrast** between them plain in the context of spiritual best practices.

Two Common Economic Systems

Economic systems differ mainly in the way they embody the spiritual practice of **equity. Equity** is demanding because it requires both individuals and organizations to be rigorous about the **fairness** of each exchange. That's much easier to do in a one-to-one relationship! Highly controlled economic theories place **equity** in the hands of a few powerful regulators; decentralized economic theories push the choice to practice **equity** (or **inequity**) to the people or organizations in each exchange. In practice, this may seem daunting, so let's start slow!

Economic systems emerge in part based on the comfort and tendencies of the people making exchanges within them. When people sustain a historical culture of interdependence and mutual reliance, their eventual political system replicates that culture. In **contrast**, when a new culture emerges, such as the emergence of America in the 17th Century, time and experimentation are part of the process to develop a sustainable political system that helps sustain the culture.

Now, let's take a close look at exactly how to accomplish the scaling-up of spiritual best practices, in the context of economic systems. For brevity, we will over-simplify with a focus on spiritual best practices within just two of the 50 or so economic systems.

- **Socialist**: people generally engage spiritual best practices, whether willingly or by manipulation or coercion, and trust a central controlling authority to use much of their treasure to provide essential common and common pool goods to all.

- **Capitalist**: people generally engage spiritual best practices, because it is in their self interest to do so in exchange of their treasure for common and common pool goods, and this trend is generally sustainable and self-healing.

Each system has its own set of strengths and shortcomings, and it is possible to skillfully co-opt each system for one's own financial benefit. Give one kid in kindergarten a candy bar, for example, and you will shortly see both types of economic systems at work as the kid tries to figure out what to do. In this context, let's ask the question: in which economic system do spiritual best practices thrive?

If the kid is a good socialist, he will share equally among the entire class (because he will get in trouble if he doesn't!). The kid will feel special for the gift of the candy bar and will of necessity consume only a small portion of the entire treat – the same size portion as everyone else. The kid might experience something about **equity** as a result.

If the kid is a good capitalist, he will probably save some of the candy bar for later (the practice of **scarcity**) while sharing the rest with the class with **equity**. He will probably be taunted for not sharing the entire treat with the class.

How does one evaluate the wisdom of either economic system with respect to spiritual best practices? This process might start with asking questions such as these to investigate the **equity** in any given exchange, from the personal to the enterprise:

- What is the **equity** in the exchange of my talent for treasure? If you volunteer your time, is that exchange equitable or fair? If you draw a salary or commission, does it adequately reward your effort without burdening the organization unfairly?

- Within your working group or team, is there **equity** in the distribution of the work? If your organization is all spooled up on culture and principles, this ought to be obvious at every level; if not, there's a worthwhile discussion to be had, specifically about the spiritual practice of **equity**.

- Looking outward from the organization, is there **equity** in its exchanges with customers or clients?

Today's awareness of income disparity and resource scarcity is worrisome. Putting treasure aside for a rainy day seems to have been taken to excess by those at the top of the food chain. It's heartening to see some of the world's billionaires give some of their treasure back in support of club goods. Does it matter much whether this is the act of a socialist or capitalist? Is it a spiritual best practice? Let's take a closer look at this trend.

Equity has a direct relationship to **sustainability**. **Sustainability** could be "having a lot of money in reserve" in case times get bad, but there's another way of practicing **sustainability**: becoming indispensible. An organization that provides health care services with **equity**, for example, might find itself with more long-term opportunities for exchange than a similar organization that does not practice **equity**.

As mentioned above, an excellent case study of this is happening in America as the nation attempts to provision health care services for all citizens. Ironically, and partly as a result of strict, centralized control (socialist), health care providers that practice **equity** seem to have also become best suited for **sustainability**. Such innovative, lower-cost not-for-profit fee-for-service providers, subscription-based clinics, and health care cost-sharing pools are beginning to enjoy more attention. Why? Because the growing social consciousness of **equity** among those who need health care no longer favors capitalist health insurance organizations' and care providers' demands for more and more treasure in exchange for less and less care. Health care consumers are, on their own, searching for better ways to obtain that care, and caregivers who practice **equity** – who offer the best care in exchange for treasure – are finding consumers they never would have found without that spiritual practice! This is an interesting example of the **resiliency** of capitalism: when things get too expensive, new options can emerge.

Which is better: the enforced **equity** of socialism or the voluntary **equity** of capitalism?

Equity, as well as all other spiritual best practices, has an attractive quality. People want to participate in it. With respect to health care, providers and patients who practice **equity** find they have quite a lot in common beyond just the demand for care and the supply of it. They learn that they can enjoy the process of exchange while minimizing or eliminating the tragedy of the commons and the **rivalrousness** and **excludability** of health care club goods. This voluntary socialism serves health care providers and consumers well because it is a spiritual best practice of **equity**.

The spiritual best practice of **equity** is also at work in the "farm to table" and "farmers' market" exchanges, where common goods (food) trade without exploitation between producers and consumers, and there is mutual **respect** for **sustainability**.

Can the **equity** of voluntary socialism scale up from individual to organization?

There may be parts of an organization or its business that don't, won't, or can't respond to or practice **equity** effectively. A good example of one such failure is the Seattle, Washington, company Gravity Payments, whose CEO decided to pay everyone employed there a minimum wage of $70,000 per year. It failed. If nothing else, this experiment weakened the company's ability to do useful work.[23] It also demonstrated that **equity** in terms of the exchange of talent and time for treasure, couldn't be imposed equally from the top. In fact, the biggest complaint employees had was that the arrangement was **unfair**.

Socialism addresses **fairness** by mandating **equity** in every exchange; capitalism addresses **fairness** by allowing individuals and organizations to determine **equity** in every exchange. **Equity**, therefore, is highly dependent on individual perception of what is **fair**. For example, if fishermen agree to limit the amount of fish caught each season so that natural replenishment takes place, they are practicing a kind of voluntary socialist **equity**. If you and I agree that the treasure I give you in exchange for the fish you give me is **fair**, we are practicing capitalist **equity**.

Before we can scale a spiritual best practice beyond the individual exchange, it's useful to understand how to effectively practice **equity** within an organization. There will be a more in-depth how-to discussion in the chapter on Implementation, so this example will be brief.

We have seen that practicing **equity** begins at the one-to-one level. In your organization, you may ask yourself questions like these:

- How do co-workers (or team members or whatever your organization calls those of us who work together) interact?

- What are their expectations of one another and of their chain of command?

- How do they treat each other on the job?

Each of these exchanges – yes: an exchange can be non-monetary – is an opportunity to practice **equity**.

Are you conscious of the demands your organization makes on the other members of your team? Do you allow that awareness to inform the language you use when speaking with them, especially when you need something they can provide? Practicing **equity** can be as easy as a considerate "when you have a chance..." preface to your request, because that lets your team member know you are offering **respect** for their talents and the other tasks on their to-do list before adding your request to it. **Equity** doesn't make demands; it's a practice that allows others to respond to your needs based on a mutual agreement that works for both. Much different than "I need this before close of business...today!!"

As each individual on the team begins to practice, **equity** can become a habit within the team, and the entire team can come to embody that spiritual best practice. Some might say that the "soul" of the team transforms through this process.

Notice that, in this discussion of the practice of **equity**, there's no mention of **scarcity** or **lack**? **Equity** is a spiritual practice that evolved because people mutually agreed that being fair with one another and thinking of their connected good with a long-term mindset worked better than a practice that resulted in furthering the tragedy of the commons – furthering the practices of **scarcity** and **lack**. This is how a practice of **equity** can trend toward **sustainability**.

Because spiritual best practices are attractive, as we keep practicing them the interest in what we're doing and why it's working can become contagious. Teams that begin to practice **equity** can extend this practice to other teams within the organization in the same way that individuals do with one another. With skillful, supportive leadership, spiritual best practices can infect the entire organization.

To conclude our discussion of economics and spiritual best practices, have you noticed that the attractive, voluntary nature of **equity** is neither socialist nor capitalist? The grass-roots trend among individuals and organizations is toward the attraction and success of "doing the right thing" and away from reliance on central control to enforce what's best for everyone. It's not really all about economic systems any more; when people and organizations adopt spiritual best practices in economics, these practices assume a recognizable, qualitative value of their own that can transcend economic systems. We've explored how this works with respect to universal health care; it will be intriguing to watch how spiritual best practices inform resolution of issues like climate change and resource depletion as diplomats are forced to move out of their comfortable economic systems and practice **equity** on the world stage.

TO SUMMARIZE

The most basic level of spiritual practice is in one's own day-to-day life. How we treat ourselves scales up to how we treat those closest to us. Practice spiritual best in your own daily routine, extend that practice to family and friends, scale that up to co-workers and organizational teams, and finally scale that up to entire organizations. Do this without circumscribing spiritual best practices to a particular level – that is, "I'll do this at home but it won't be acceptable at the office!" – and it becomes possible to create sustainable, energetic, positive movement that is attractive to other individuals and organizations. Research in organizational best practice supports the wisdom of this approach; now, we can finally call those best practices what they actually are: the discovery and realization of the spirit – the essential self – of the organization.

CHAPTER FOUR

IMPLEMENTATION: HOW DO I DO THIS?

T his Chapter will focus on the how-to of implement-
ing spiritual best practices. We have touched on how
spiritual best practices start at the individual level of
personal practice and relationships, then scale to families
and teams, then eventually to enterprises, and we have seen
some examples of how strong leadership can influence the
spread of culture and principles. Let's examine the specifics
of spiritual best practice as they infect an organization, and
how to supercharge that process.

While these simple steps are scalable from individual
up to a team or organization level, the process begins with
your own spiritual practices. Take an inventory of them;
decide which ones serve you and which ones don't; change
the ones that don't serve you. Repeat. Master this on the
personal level and you can scale it up to apply to relationship, team, organization. Ready?

Here's how the process works:

1. Make an accounting of the spiritual practices
    you are doing now;

2. Evaluate those practices within your culture;

3. Evaluate those practices within your principles;

4. Evaluate those practices within your brand;

5. Evaluate those practices within your relationships.

Once you can do this with your individual spiritual practices, you will be ready to scale the process to your family, team, and organization. We will provide action items for each step along the way, and some assistance in the scaling-up process. Yes: there's a reason the process starts and ends with you: often it's easier to recognize what's "out there" than what's "in here." Ready?

SPIRITUAL THINGS YOU'RE ALREADY DOING

To begin, take stock of the spiritual best practices you use already as a normal part of care for yourself. What are some of them? Take a moment to write down as many personal spiritual best practices as you can – ones you practice regularly. Your list might resemble an inventory of good habits. If you're uncertain about a particular term, use it in a short sentence, such as "The spiritual best practice of _____." Your list may include some of the ones mentioned in this book such as the ones listed below (save yourself some time and just highlight the ones in your personal toolkit), or it may include many others we haven't yet discussed. You may find yourself adding to the list during some of the next steps; that's OK.

A Sample List of Spiritual Best Practices

Appreciation	Respect	Kindness	Consistency
Discretion	Loyalty	Humility	Honor
Resilience	Authenticity	Empathy	Humor
Integrity	Mentoring	Vision	Excellence
Equity	Courage	Abundance	Contrast
Dialogue	Compromise	Altruism	Cooperation
Collaboration	Ethics	Fairness	Compassion
Dignity	Deliberation	Patience	Sustainability

You may find yourself listing spiritual practices that aren't "best" or about which you can't make a distinction – at this point, do so without judgment – it will be OK later. For completeness and later reference, here's table of contrasting opposite practices to the spiritual bests listed above:

A Sample List of Spiritual "Worst" Practices

Neglect	Disrespect	Unkindness	Inconsistency
Indiscretion	Disloyalty	Arrogance	Dishonor
Rigidity	Incompetence	Disdain	Drama
Deceit	Inhibiting	Blindness	Imperfection
Bias	Cowardice	Lack	Conformity
Monologue	Dissent	Meanness	Antagonism
Division	Corruption	Partiality	Cruelty
Insignificance	Carelessness	Agitation	Waste

Your list doesn't have to be a long one – you will know it's complete when it feels natural. You can always add to or modify it later. Nothing about spiritual best practices needs to be forced – in fact, it's counterproductive to try to enforce a spiritual best practice.

> ➢ **Action Item:** create a list of the spiritual practices you already use. (If you are doing this as a team, everyone participates – whiteboard the results for everyone to see.) Call this list "My/Our Spiritual Practices."

As you review your list, do you find there are practices you wish you did better? Practices you wish you didn't use at all? Practices you aren't sure about? Do you find there are practices that are important to you but unwelcome to others? This exercise demands a certain amount of introspection; discovery and realization of your inner spirit engages the kind of deep "soul" work that is an essential part of spiritual practice.

Keep that list handy – you will need it for the next steps.

STRENGTH TO YOUR CULTURE

Have you ever considered your personal culture the way you might have thought about the culture of the organization(s) in which you participate? Now that you have your list of spiritual practices, ask yourself these questions:

- Does this list trend toward best practices, or not?

- How do the practices listed help me/us in life?

- How do the practices listed hinder me/us in life?

- Do I/we use these practices universally, or do I/we employ different ones in personal life than in participation on the job?

To sort out your answers to these questions, you may find it helpful to use a separate sheet of paper (or page in a digital document); write each spiritual practice on your original list at the top of a blank page, and follow it with your answers to the questions above. Here's the complete action item:

➢ **Action Item:** write each of the spiritual practices you already use on its own page, then answer these questions about each practice:

- *Is this a spiritual best practice or not?*

- *How does this spiritual practice help?*

- *How does this spiritual practice hinder?*

- *Do I/we use this practice universally, only in personal life, only on the job, or some combination?*

It's not uncommon to inhabit two different cultures: a personal one and an organizational one. This was not always the case.

The culture that sustained IBM until the 1980s was one that scooped up and surrounded the families of people who worked there. Military culture tends to do the same, as do some trade unions. Workers in those kinds of organizations subordinate their personal culture – and in many ways, the personal culture of their families and friends – to the culture of the organization. Often, people who choose to work in such organizations do so for the benefit of the strong organizational culture, and welcome its effect on their personal lives. If the organizational culture trends toward spiritual best practices, this can enliven and invigorate the personal cultures of the people who participate in it, even outside the day-to-day of the organization. This historic trend, however, has shifted.

More and more, people have de-coupled their personal lives from the organizations in which they earn their livelihood. Companies no longer "own" their employees the way they once did. Improving our individual, personal culture matters, perhaps more than ever before,[24] and we consume vast quantities of "how-to" material at an alarming rate. Clearly, people want to build their individual cultures in ways that are sustainable.

The list of spiritual practices you have made offers you a starting point. As you answer the questions posed about it, you may notice practices that don't serve you – practices that interfere with the culture of sustainability that you want for yourself.

For example, thanks to a long family history, I happen to have become an expert in passive aggression. This is not a spiritual best practice! On the other hand, it was an ingrained part of my personal culture, and I used it effectively. That worked well enough...until my personal culture began to include people I really cared for who wouldn't tolerate me being passive aggressive. At this point, I realized that passive aggression wasn't sustainable in my personal culture, and that I was the one who had to change. I had to learn to replace my practice of passive aggression with a best spiritual practice: I had to learn **assertion** without **aggression**.

As you check your list against what works in your culture, you may find there are tweaks needed to align your personal practices with what works better for you personally and professionally. No judgment here; it's just a matter of recognizing how your culture serves you...or not. If not, identify the practices that don't serve you and replace them with better ones.

Yes: it's called "practice" for a good reason. We humans are generally fairly good at learning new stuff, provided we don't resist too much or allow ourselves to get comfortable with "the way it's always been done," especially when that way no longer serves us best.

Culture is malleable. It changes and adapts as necessary. Cultural changes aren't something to fear; culture *must* evolve if an individual or organization is to adapt to external changes and continue to thrive. Think of a family making the transitions required to raise kids from infants to adults; the culture of the family naturally changes to support the kids as they mature and the parents as they learn and practice new parenting skills. We're supposed to be able to do this!

While culture and the practices we bring to it change, principles are the fixed foundation that grounds us.

STRENGTH TO YOUR PRINCIPLES

When you ask yourself those introspective questions about your spiritual practices list you'll quickly find there are gray areas. How do we know what's best when a spiritual practice could also be used in the worst possible way? Our principles, hopefully, guide us toward the best practice.

Manipulation is one such practice that falls into a gray area. Let's explore this first in the realm of fantasy, where real lives aren't at stake.

When you see a movie, you tacitly agree to allow the entertainment to manipulate you. We generally agree that this is acceptable best practice. Would you see a movie that left you feeling flat, bored or indifferent? We expect entertainment to manipulate us. One principle behind the practice of **manipulation** in entertainment might be "do no harm;" even though the movie was terrifying, we submitted to it with the knowledge that, while me might have a bad dream or two, the terror in the movie is imaginary. We might call this a principled use of **manipulation** as a spiritual best practice that does no harm.

On the other hand, **manipulation** practiced with a harmful or selfish intent is a dishonest way to change behavior or obtain an objective, such as when a manager **manipulates** a team member through **threat** or **deceit** to produce an outcome.

For this example, which spiritual practice of **manipulation** is truly "best?" Hopefully, your answer takes the underlying principle into account: the best spiritual practice of **manipulation** is the one that does no harm. Often, in organizations, a short-term objective crowds out the spiritual best practice, and it takes a courageous team or manager to stay committed to the underlying principles of the organization.

Principles guide individuals and organizations. For example, the principle "do not kill" animates people and organizations whose mission is peace, or health care, or suicide intervention. No person or organization with a mission of peace will tolerate practices that permit killing. It's obvious that entirely different principles are in play in military service, where taking human life is part of the objective. Can you imagine how this **contrast** causes personal distress for warriors?

Your personal principles usually align with your personal beliefs. Most of us subscribe to some well-known and/or widely acceptable belief system, whether religious, scientific, political, or economic. It matters not so much what those principles are, but that you – or your organization – have them. Deeply held individual principles often propel us to align with – or work for – organizations that share those same principles; it's a source of great **contrast** to find oneself in a conversation or organization that doesn't share the principles that are dear to us, and that response is completely normal. We will address the navigation of that **contrast** in the section on strengthening relationships; what's important now is that you have a clear understanding of the principles that underlie your personal or organizational culture.

Organizations generally advertise their principles in a public mission statement. Here are some examples for consideration. Which one speaks most clearly to you of the strength of the organization's culture? You saw the first one earlier in this book; the other for-profit examples given here are from the excellent website Strategic Management Insight,[25] which evaluates mission statements based on a number of recognized criteria. The not-for-profit mission statements come from the web pages cited.

For-Profit Organizations
sammysoap

"sammysoap is a job creation machine for adults with intellectual disabilities *disguised* as the world's best soap company. We are not a not-for-profit, on purpose. We manage to the strengths of our employees to make the best soap around. We exist in support of human health, a clean planet, and **disability wage equality**."

The Coca Cola Company

"Our mission is: To refresh the world in mind, body and spirit. To inspire moments of optimism and happiness through our brands and actions."

IBM

Since 2003, IBM hasn't had an official mission statement. Instead, it translates company purpose through values.

IBMers value:

- Dedication to every client's success

- Innovation that matters – for our company and for the world

- Trust and personal responsibility in all relationships

Not-For-Profit Organizations
Wounded Warrior Project
"To honor and empower Wounded Warriors."[26]

Rotary International
"The mission of Rotary International is to provide service to others, promote integrity, and advance world understanding, goodwill, and peace through its fellowship of business, professional, and community leaders."[27]

San Diego Veterans Coalition
"The SDVC is a catalyst that inspires collaboration and cooperation among service partners to deliver

premier support for Veterans in the San Diego region."[28]

Which mission statements speak to *you* of the principles that underlie the organization? Based on the principles in their mission statements, would you consider joining any of them? There are no wrong answers here; this is a way for you to discover how your personal principles stack up against a few organizational ones. Whether or not you are familiar with these organizations, can you make any value judgments about their success relative to their stated missions? In general, there is usually a connection between the clarity of an organization's principles and the reputation and success of that organization, just as that connection exists for each of us as individuals.

Now, which of the organizations we've sampled here do you think might have the best spiritual practices? For individuals, the clearer our principles, the more astute we are at spiritual practices. The same holds true for organizations. Here are some of my observations:

- sammysoap is clear about its principles: human health, a clean planet, and disability wage equality. That's powerful.

- Coca Cola is very clear about its principles: optimism and happiness. It's also quite clear about how those principles are put into practice: to refresh the world in mind, body and spirit. A+.

- Could the erosion of IBM's market share be related to its missing mission statement? It's not enough to just share your values with the world; the world needs to know *how you practice those values* and why. **Dedication**, **trust**, **innovation** and personal **responsibility** are certainly spiritual best practices, but what are the underlying principles?

- Could Wounded Warrior Project have steered around its negative publicity with a mission statement that, though lofty, contains more substance?

- Rotary International also gets an A+ for being clear with its principles: integrity, understanding, goodwill, and peace.

- San Diego Veterans Coalition embodies the spiritual best practices of **collaboration** and **cooperation**, but it's missing clearly stated guiding principles.

It's not difficult to write a mission statement when culture and principles are clear. We are steering around value judgments here; your culture and principles are *yours* regardless of how anyone else feels about them, and your objective is to be as clear and pithy about them as possible. To do this, you're going to condense it all into your very own mission statement. This isn't always easy and you may make a few tries and have a few rough drafts to consider before you decide on one – be **patient** and **persistent** and the process will have its reward.

> ➢ **Action Item:** Based on your spiritual practices and your introspective answers to the questions about each one, compose your personal (or team, or organization) mission statement

Now it's time to leverage your mission statement into the face you or your organization show to the world: your brand.

STRENGTH TO YOUR BRAND

If your name is your brand, you get a pass on this part of the process. For most of us, and especially for organizations, that's not always the case. Whether you're re-invigorating a long-standing brand, as IBM has done, or creating a new one, the steps are the same.

To begin with the end in mind is always a good idea. Let's use one of my favorite organizations as an example: People Assisting the Homeless (PATH). It's simple to find PATH's mission statement because it's on almost every page of the PATH website (see http://www.epath.org):

> "PATH is ending homelessness for individuals, families, and communities. We do this by building housing and providing supportive services throughout California."

While PATH doesn't need to advertise the spiritual best practices behind their mission, we immediately understand that "ending homelessness" for PATH is not just about warehousing people: PATH approaches homelessness holistically with both a home and supportive services to raise every part of its clients' living standards. The mission statement has an implied sense that PATH understands what it is like to "come home" and that this involves more than just a front door. Behind and between the lines of its mission we can see PATH's spiritual best practices, such as **dignity**, **respect**, **kindness**, **empathy**, and **compassion** at work. PATH is a tax-advantaged organization, which implies that it also practices **sustainability** and **altruism**, as well as **courage** and **patience**. PATH incorporated in 1984, and it has a history of working alongside other organizations and community groups, so it must practice **sustainability** and **collaboration**, too.

A not-for-profit at work for thirty years on a problem that just keeps getting bigger is a worthwhile organization! Because donors are extremely savvy when it comes to how their treasure is used by tax-advantaged organizations, PATH's longevity isn't accidental. If PATH didn't practice **authenticity, integrity,** and **consistency**, donors would have abandoned it long ago.

All this…and we have yet to actually discuss the things PATH does to end homelessness! By unpacking PATH's mission statement we are able to take a peek at the principles behind the practices – the organization's "morality," if you will – and learn a bit about the culture of the organization itself. In very broad terms, PATH's culture is built around "doing the right thing" to end homelessness, and PATH has done that in part by incorporating spiritual best practices into its culture.

PATH was clever about its name, because the services PATH offers follow so seamlessly from its acronym. That is PATH's brand, and its trademarked logo pulls everything together:

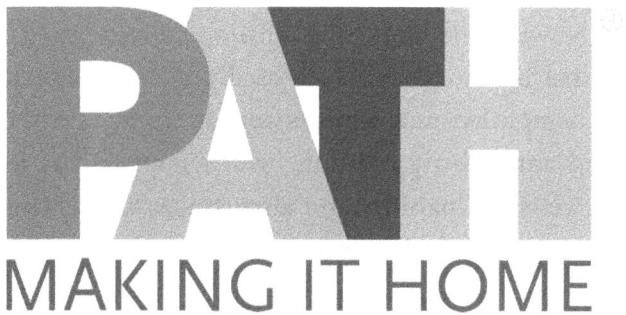

MAKING IT HOME

This is brilliant branding in so many ways: the double entendre of "making it home;" the movement of color from red "P" through the green "A" and violet "T" to the stability of the blue capital "H" (toward "home"); the implied pathway or journey home. Does PATH's brand reflect its mission (culture and principles)? Absolutely.

What about your brand?

There's no reason why individuals can't have a personal brand, but it's still easier for us to be objective about an organization's brand instead of a person's. Even so, a quick look at some successful personal brands might be useful:

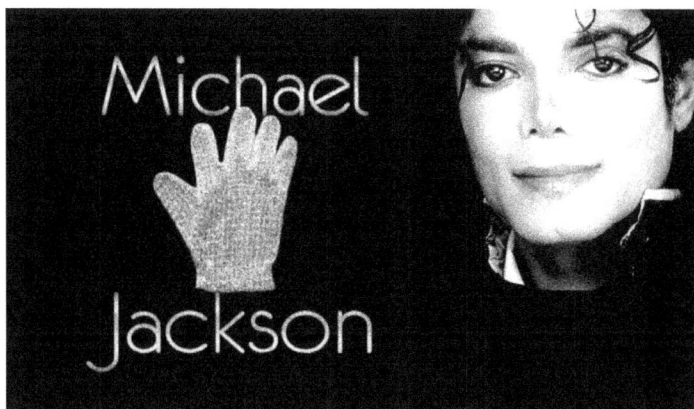

Your brand – the public face you or your organization show the world – can almost seem like it's a real person, separate from you. Each of the brands shown here stands for something unique and far bigger in many ways than the actual, living person behind the brand. From the dynasties of the Dali Lama or the Queen of England to the profound music, sporting goods, and entrepreneurial influences of Jackson, Jordan and Kay, there is something at work that's much bigger than the person or even the persona. How do we get into *that*?

If you've been doing the work so far, you have written a mission statement (either personal or organizational), supported by your list of spiritual practices and introspective questions about each practice. Strengthening your brand is all about consciously enhancing the flavor of your brand to be consistent with the mission and spiritual best practices behind it *as everyone except you sees it*. Simply put:

Your brand is how the world sees you.

That means, very simply, that you can have a snazzy logo, tag line, website, and all the rest of the marketing pieces in place, but if the world doesn't clearly see you (or your organization) the way you believe the world ought to, there's a problem with your brand.

Fortunately, the solution is easy. It takes a little work, but it's work worth doing well.

Consider the way you or your organization are perceived by your friends, clients or customers, family, colleagues or co-workers, and significant others. Social media tends to make this easier, since you can quickly ask a reasonably large number of people for their perspective. Remember, your brand is about how others see you, and you can't determine if your brand is working without asking others about it.

> **Action Item:** Ask for feedback. Contact your friends, family, team, customers, clients, co-workers, colleagues with an open-ended questionnaire or survey about yourself or your organization and ask them to respond to questions like these:

  · *What do you perceive to be my/our <u>strengths</u>?*

  · *What do you perceive to be my/our <u>weaknesses</u>?*

  · *If I/we could improve one or two areas about <u>how I/we interact</u> with you, what would those be?*

  · *What is the most important thing I/we could be doing for you or with you that we aren't yet doing? Why is that important to you?*

Whether you have an existing brand or are developing one from scratch, the results you get back will tell you why you must strengthen that brand. Whether you've done this type of exercise before or not, the important thing is <u>how</u> you will do that. That is, if you get feedback that you're sometimes too pushy and impatient, this is an indication that your brand needs to embody more **humor**, **kindness** and **patience.**

> ➤ **Action Item:** In the responses you receive, search carefully for terms that indicate spiritual practice, whether best or "worst." Do this as much as possible without defensiveness or value judgment!

> ➤ **Action Item:** Gather the "best" terms into a stand-alone list. Compare this list against the spiritual best practices you first wrote down. Add anything new to your original list!

> ➤ **Action Item:** Gather the "worst" terms into a stand-alone list, then:

> - *Do any of these "worst" terms have an opposite spiritual "best" practice already on your original list? If so, highlight that opposite "best" practice as a place to spend more of your energy, because you just learned that the spiritual best practice you thought you were doing isn't coming through clearly in your brand!*

> - *Do any of these "worst" terms have an opposite spiritual best practice that's not on your original list? Add the spiritual best practice to your original list and start doing more of that in your brand!*

At this point, you will also have some insight into your personal (or team's or organization's) principles. It can be scary when a customer or client calls you out for being unethical or even unfair, but the evidence seems to indicate that best spiritual practices in these fundamental areas are what sets success apart from failure. Honestly, can you really expect that treating customers unfairly will keep them coming back?

> **Action Item:** Re-check your mission statement to make certain it still aligns with your original (or modified!) list of best spiritual practices. If not, revise it!

If you're paying close attention, you may have concluded that the effect of all this work is to bring your inward best spiritual practice into alignment with your outward-facing best spiritual practice. Individuals and organizations with this kind of alignment are the ones that are most **authentic** and **consistent**, which also makes the perception of their brand **reliable**. These are the organizations that "do the right thing," from delivering the most amazing services and products to caring for their team members, and – usually – you will find that the individuals in those organizations practice the same kind of **integrity**.

Strength to Your Relationships

Before we move on, please know that the exercise of integrating spiritual best practices into an organization can be disruptive, just as my transformation of passive aggression to assertion was disruptive for me as I learned a new way of being. The results of that disruption were worth it; no reason they can't be worth it for you and your organization, too.

Up to this point, everything we've discussed is one step removed from *you*. With relationships, the notion of spiritual best practices comes home to each of us and becomes actionable. What does it look like and feel like in the real, messy world to actually practice **authenticity, integrity,** or **consistency**? What practices do you or your organization embrace that are authentic, integral, and consistent? Are you already doing this? Just beginning? Never considered it before? This is where it all starts, and it can start now.

Remember the table of sample spiritual best practices?

Appreciation	Respect	Kindness	Consistency
Discretion	Loyalty	Humility	Honor
Resilience	Authenticity	Empathy	Humor
Integrity	Mentoring	Vision	Excellence
Equity	Courage	Abundance	Contrast
Dialogue	Compromise	Altruism	Cooperation
Collaboration	Ethics	Fairness	Compassion
Dignity	Deliberation	Patience	Sustainability

Your objective is to put each spiritual best practice into action, so here are some real examples of how to do that. If this language is new, memorize it, and use it...a lot. These examples use the spiritual best practices from the top row:

- "Thank you. I really *appreciate* your quick response on that project."

- "I *respect* your time and expertise, and it would help me a lot if you would spend a few minutes discussing this project."

- "It was really *kind* of you to show me that study – really helped me with this assignment."

- "Our team's track record is so *consistent*: one home run after another – nice job everyone!"

Now, you give it a try. Remember: the idea is not just to use the word, but to tie it in to a specific action. That's practice. Write down your responses – that's how they become real – memorize them, and *use them.* If you have added other spiritual best practices to your list, that's fine; try it with these first then move on to the others.

Discretion

_____
_____
_____

Loyalty

_____
_____
_____

Humility

_____

_____

_____

Honor

_____

_____

_____

If you noticed that those spiritual best practices really made you think hard about how to do them, you're doing it correctly; you *want* to thoughtfully consider to how to personalize each one.

Here are my responses to the same spiritual best practices – notice how the spiritual best practice can happen without always relying on the specific term?

- **Discretion:** "Thank you for explaining this to me – I can see how it really helps us make progress. Glad to keep the information between us until the big announcement."

- **Loyalty:** "Just wanted you to know: no plans to bail out on the team during this crisis. I'm in, whatever it takes."

- **Humility:** "Yeah, I've still got my opinions, but I'll set them aside so all of us can move forward and finish this project."

- **Honor:** "I understand how important your project is for all of us. Let me arrange for some extra bandwidth to help move the ball."

(You could try this same exercise on a personal relationship level, of course, but we will keep our focus on you as a member of an organization.)

Do you see that there's more than one way to implement each spiritual best practice? If so, you're doing the work well. The idea to grasp is that the "right" way to do spiritual best practice might vary, but the core concept – the specific spiritual best practice – remains the same. For example, there are many ways to show **appreciation**, and the ways that work best and seem most natural to you may be different from the way anyone else shows or expresses **appreciation**. That's completely and perfectly appropriate. This is *not* a "one size fits all" thing.

You may also notice that there's a difference between spiritual best and spiritual not-so-best practice. That is, **discretion** is a spiritual best practice when used to keep confidence around preparations for a big product announcement but not, for example, when covering up illegal action by the organization. In the second case, it's still the spiritual practice of **discretion**, and, while it might be "best" to be part of the cover-up at that moment, that practice might also result in jail time. While the action is virtually identical, there's a big difference between the implications and potential results of those two practices of **discretion**!

As you become more adept at spiritual practices, you may also begin to notice a difference in the energy around them. Generally, a spiritual not-best practice will feel less than satisfying, maybe slightly questionable, like something is a bit off but you're not sure exactly what. A spiritual best practice will have a good, satisfying, more confident energy or feeling around it – it will feel more authentically "right." This is because spiritual best practices tend to align more with universal ethics than with situational morality or value judgment.

There's no pass/fail test for spiritual best practices in relationship. This means you're going to have to trust yourself to try different ways of using spiritual practices until you find the ones that feel best for you. The results and responses you get from your practice will help guide you. If you are getting good results this means the practice is working, and you can begin to test whether or not it is "best." As we mentioned above, there's more than one right way to do this. This also means that, as you scale individual practice up to the team and organization level, you're not going to be able to write a successful policy or script to dictate exactly how to practice spiritual best. Recall our earlier discussions on culture, principles, and brand? Spiritual practices are intrinsic to culture, principles, and brand expressed in the day-to-day actions and interactions of the organization and in the products or services the organization provides. We evaluate whether or not those practices are "best" based either on our own fluency with them, or on the organization's public-facing qualitative appearance. Yes: there's a certain level of "trust your gut" here, and you will find that your engagement with individual spiritual best practices in your one-to-one relationships automatically helps you become more aware of them on a team or organizational scale, and that, with exercise, your radar for successful spiritual best practices will become quite accurate.

Please, be kind! Awareness of spiritual best practices comes with an obligation of **patience** toward those who don't yet get it, and all of us grow in the talent of spiritual best practice at different rates. It's up to each one of us to encourage our peers to become fluent in spiritual best practices at whatever speed works best for them.

Mentoring

Mentoring may be the very best arena for an individual or organization to nurture spiritual best practices. What spiritual best practices help make a mentor? Mentors often walk into the unknown with **confidence** because they understand that their spiritual best practices work between people regardless of the situation or talents of the protégé. I have been a protégé to C-level executives and homeless people alike, so I've had to learn that **authenticity** can sit in the corner office or on the street. One of my most successful protégés may not live to see publication of this book, but has found a new peace and contentment with life he didn't think possible before our work together. There's no guidebook for such situations, but spiritual best practices such as **appreciation**, **respect**, **kindness**, **humor**, **loyalty**, **empathy**, and especially **humility** are enough to make such relationships work, and work well. **Mentoring** isn't about having all the answers; it's about **consistency** in the face of questions: standing beside a protégé as they face the unknown; keeping the **dialogue** open for **deliberation**; offering **integrity**; discovering each other's **resilience**; allowing **vision** and **contrast** to work. Often, the spiritual best practice of **mentoring** rewards the mentor just as richly as it rewards the protégé.

Contrast

When relationships sour, as they often do, we can experience truly uncomfortable **contrast**. How can spiritual best practices guide us through times where **disagreement** is necessary?

We need **contrast** to evaluate, discuss, decide, and often to learn. One scientist found that rote memorization is not as powerful as the Socratic method of question and answer[29] when it comes to the best way for humans to learn. Something about us is just hardwired to grok new data better when it results from question and answer. **Contrast** is one spiritual best practice that's well suited for this process, especially when individuals are searching together for a pathway to **equity**. Yes, this does involve **compromise**, but it also may require **dissent, resistance,** and **argument**. (If you're paying attention, you might notice that those terms appear for the first time here as spiritual best practices.)

How can **dissent, resistance,** and **argument** be spiritual best practices? Like many such questions, the answer depends on how they are used. In our American Congress, for example, the rules by which bills become laws promote **dialogue** resulting in **compromise**. If the **dialogue** happens with **dignity, humility,** and perhaps **empathy** and even **humor**, it can be quite productive. Sadly, this isn't often the case, even though the Congressional rules have their origins in many centuries of positive evidence that such spiritual practices are in fact best.

It's a real benefit for we human beings to be skilled at **dissent, resistance**, and **argument**, and to discharge them with **dignity, humility, empathy,** and **humor**. Historically, when we do that, great things happen, from scientific advances to solutions to huge social and political issues. When humankind fails to do so, bad things happen. War, poverty, and worldwide despair can result when spiritual practices are abused or ignored on the world stage, but let's keep this closer to home and think about how things work in one-to-one relationships within a team.

While we celebrate individual creativity and invention and the talent that goes with it, human beings are at their collective best solving problems innovatively and cooperatively. From business or marriage partners to inter-governmental initiatives, the spirit of **cooperation** in the solutions to what ails us often arise from two or more people or organizations working together. **Dissent** and **argument** are useful spiritual best practice tools for sorting through options to find the one that fits the problem perfectly. The object lesson here is to embrace these more difficult spiritual practices without taking personal offense, and that *does* take practice! The aphorism "agree to disagree" is real-life evidence of this practice: parties to an argument who hold each other's standpoints in high regard and allow themselves to continue the **contrast** until a workable compromise is reached often achieve the best results.

And when things go really wrong? **Patience** in the face of threats isn't easy, and **humor** may not always be the most appropriate practice to open a way forward, but skillful negotiators, legislators, and managers can usually find a way to keep the energy of healthy **contrast** alive until an obvious solution appears.

When one-to-one team relationships break down, the crisis that results can often trigger new ideas and novel ways forward. The spiritual best practice of **acceptance**, even in the face of a crisis, speeds this process. Again, no one wants to create a crisis, but if that happens, it can sometimes be the shortest route to a solution, provided you are willing to actively practice **dignity**, **humility, empathy,** and **humor**, or whatever applicable spiritual best practices are in your comfort zone. Organizations that resolve internal and external crises in this way are the models for organizations that wish they could, and since these practices happen at the one-to-one level and are scalable, there's hope and inspiration in this kind of transformative process, wouldn't you agree?

As you influence each of your relationships based on your intrinsic qualities, so does an organization influence each of its business-to-business relationships based on its culture, principles and brand. Researchers are finding that, as in human relationships, businesses prefer to exchange with other businesses whose culture, principles and brand have commonalities.[30] Just as in inter-personal relationships, businesses discover those commonalities by reputation and experience, as well as in the public-facing information they display to each other.

TWEAK YOUR PUBLIC-FACING LANGUAGE

What do your resume or personal online profile(s) say about you? How **authentic** are you? Are you honest about yourself in the social media face you show the world? If you show the world a personal philosophy or call to action online, how closely does it resemble your core beliefs? I'm being rhetorical here to make the point: Just as our personal relationships take some time to develop and reach a new degree of authenticity, so too do our organizations need time to evolve their interactions with the world. Organizations in their early stages often project lofty, untested goals and ambitions; more seasoned organizations tend to offer a more reasonable public-facing image supported by historical measurements. Both types of public image are valid – no judgment here – and, because it's important to the organization practicing its spiritual best to be **authentic**, both can have **integrity**. Whether an organization is brand-new or seasoned, the language it offers the world may or may not include spiritual best practices. If not, just tweak the language; that's the first step towards positively differentiating the organization.

From the mission statements we've seen above, which one offers us the best clues about the spiritual practices of the organization? Maybe it's the one with some of the spiritual best practices terms built right in? Look back on the mission statements we reviewed earlier as we evaluate them. As you will see, they aren't rich in the language of spiritual best practices! We will review a few of them.

- sammysoap has a noble purpose, and its mission statement speaks to that fact: jobs for people who wouldn't be able to get them otherwise. The word "equality" is potentially strong as a spiritual best practice, and there's an implication of **equity** in the statement "we manage to the strengths of our employees" which is very bold, considering the company exists to employ people with intellectual disabilities. I want to know more about the process of doing business with sammysoap and whether it treats its customers and suppliers with the same **honor** that it offers its employees.

- Coca Cola has a lofty mission statement. It feels good to read it! I want to know more about how it feels to work there. Are Coca Cola employees optimistic? Happy? Even momentarily? I want to know if Coca Cola practices its mission internally. Based on the success of its products, it has certainly done something right for a long time; maybe its mission statement is an **authentic** clue to what that something might be.

- Wounded Warrior Project's mission statement is clear about **honor** for those it serves, but doesn't reveal how it accomplishes that. Kudos for making the "why" obvious (**honor**), but absent a "how" (insert spiritual best practice here) it is also only half baked.

• Rotary International offers several spiritual best practice possibilities in its mission statement: "provide service," "promote **integrity**," "advance...**understanding, goodwill,** and **peace.**" Like the sammysoap mission statement, Rotary International's makes me want to know more.

A public-facing mission statement is a very constrained place to launch an organization's spiritual best practices into the world, but it's the first place to start, and an organization committed to spiritual best practices can signal that in its mission statement. This is not to say that organizations that don't offer spiritual best practices in their mission statement or other public relations materials don't practice their spiritual best! Instead, it's to encourage organizations and individuals who want to make that differentiation to do so. Why? Because the research anticipates success for organizations that do so, especially in terms of employee engagement and business to business interaction.[31]

To illustrate how a mission statement can be easily modified to include spiritual best practices, let's start with a very bare-bones example and work it into a spiritual best practices powerhouse. Here, again, is the mission statement from People Assisting the Homeless (PATH):

"PATH is ending homelessness for individuals, families, and communities. We do this by building housing and providing supportive services throughout California."

Great mission! It's clear. Obvious. But it's missing one big thing. Just like Wounded Warrior Project, it's only half-baked. Unlike Wounded Warrior Project's strong emphasis on "why," PATH is fairly strong with a practical "how." With great respect for PATH, which probably worked long and hard on its mission statement, we can improve its mission statement even more by including language of spiritual best practice.

This is not to suggest that PATH doesn't already use spiritual best practices in the way they conduct business and interact with their clients and donors! If we could sit down with PATH and discuss it, we might learn that they evaluated a number of mission statements before choosing the one they use, and that some of those might have had aspects of spiritual best practices in them. This is only an example of what could be done. Again: studies favor the success of organizations that make their spiritual best practices obvious, so we're going to mess with the PATH mission statement to do exactly that.

People generally understand that being homeless is not nice, and that "doing the right thing" to end homelessness is a noble aspiration. Can we transform PATH's mission statement to specifically include "doing the right thingness" in it? What spiritual best practices might convey that message? Using the table we've already seen twice, we could suggest PATH incorporate spiritual best practices such as **respect**, **kindness**, **dignity**, and perhaps most importantly **sustainability** into its mission.

Why?

As a donor, wouldn't you want to know that the treasure you give to PATH is used wisely? That's **sustainability** isn't it? You'd also want to know that the housing and supportive services PATH provides are given to homeless people with **respect** and **dignity**, and offered with **kindness**. If I'm scanning through the financials of organizations like PATH to determine which one to assist, I might find that all of them are quite similar, but if the mission statement speaks to me of spiritual best practices, that could be the trigger that helps me decide where to provide treasure.

As a homeless person, wouldn't I want to experience **respect**, **kindness**, and **dignity** from an organization that helps me out? Wouldn't I want to find **sustainability** in my own life as I transition from homeless to housed? If I'm facing a choice between a homeless warehouse and an organization that offers me those best spiritual practices, where do you think I might go?

Do you see how important it is to recognize spiritual best practices right up front?

How could PATH potentially strengthen it mission statement? By incorporating spiritual terms.

Incorporate Spiritual Terms

As we have seen, spiritual terms aren't necessarily the high-flying language one might hear in church. Spiritual terms tend to be down-to-earth attributes of how we express ourselves – the "flavor" of an interaction rather than the action itself.

PATH, for example, is quite good at what it does. It has years of success and good solid measurements to back up its mission statement. PATH *is* "ending homelessness for individuals, families, and communities." From its mission statement, we don't really know how PATH does that other than "building housing and providing supportive services" and there's absolutely nothing wrong with that! The suggestion here is that PATH might take its organization to the next level of success, just as other organizations are beginning to do more and more, if PATH was clear and up-front about its spiritual best practice "how."

This "how" is implied, as we have seen, in PATH's "doing the right thing" for homeless people, and we have unpacked that "right thing" to some of its specific spiritual best practice possibilities: **respect**, **kindness**, **dignity**, and **sustainability**. Now it's time to include those in PATH's new mission statement. You'll be surprised how easy this is!

If we assume here that PATH's success is due in part to the hidden "how" that's not revealed in the original mission statement, it's easy to revise it to make spiritual best practices obvious and up-front:

> "PATH ends homelessness for individuals, families, and communities throughout California. We do this by building **sustainable** housing and providing supportive services with **respect**, **kindness**, and **dignity**."

The revised mission statement implies two important things that the original mission statement did not:

1. PATH has a commitment to housing that is **sustainable,** which indicates that a) donors'

treasure is used wisely, and b) a transitioning homeless person would be able to afford to live there for some time;

2. PATH treats its clients, suppliers, employees and donors with **respect, kindness,** and **dignity.** Most homeless people aren't treated with **respect, kindness,** and **dignity,** and an organization that puts these spiritual best practices front and center makes a bold and necessary statement to the world about precisely why it is different and successful.

Remove Terms Contrary to Best Practices

All the spiritual best practice you can pack into your personal life, team, and organization are useless if they are undercut by spiritual practices that aren't best. The process of making spiritual best practices obvious is easy and forward-focused; excising spiritual worst practices can be difficult. Often, the worst aspects of oneself or one's organization resist discovery.

Contrast is a useful way to uncover the difference between best and worst practices. If your organization is short on **appreciation**, it may take **courage** to begin its best practice. **Apathy** and **indifference** are tough to replace with **inspiration** and **engagement** but there is plenty of business literature available that documents the wisdom of doing so.[B] We have all heard the "walk the talk" adage, and

---

B   See Further Reading for my favorite examples

that wisdom certainly applies here. It can also save you a lot of additional reading time.

To break it down, if your talk sucks, so will your walk: if you say you're committed to spiritual best practice and your walk doesn't reflect that, you can start to change by changing what you say. If you can be conscious of the spiritual "worst" practice words in your vocabulary (remember there's a non-exhaustive table of them earlier in this book?) then you can choose other words to replace them from the spiritual best practices table. To make it easy, the tables are set up so that the words in the same row and column of each are the opposites of each other. Doing that is a great step toward spiritual best practice and away from the opposite.

To take this from individual to organizational "walk," you may get interested enough in an organization's public information to scan it quickly for spiritual terms. While there may not be many, as we have seen from the mission statements we've examined, ask yourself: are the ones I found "best" or "worst?" If you find any of the "worst" ones, can you determine if those practices are also part of the organization's culture, principles, or brand?

Often, organizations that "have always done it this way" have deeply-ingrained practices that can't or won't change and may not be best. To see this clearly can cause us to question how our continued participation in them may or may not be sustainable over the long term. Organizations that are newer or more nimble may simply be more capable of the transformational tweaks needed to put them into spiritual best practices mode.

It can be scary to discover that an organization is devoid of spiritual best practices, but it's a good thing to know. If that's your organization, and you are in a position to enliven it with the ideas in this book, please do!

ROLL IT OUT!

Once you and your team have examined your spiritual best practice fluency, made the necessary tweaks to public-facing language, and agreed that walking the talk at this new level of best practices is the future of your organization, it's time to make that a bold public statement and join the quiet transformation already in progress. The trend toward spiritual best practice is well established. The big question is: when and how will your team join the movement?

It's not enough to just make some changes in the advertising and PR around your personal or organizational brand. We've seen how unethical people and organizations abuse spiritual best practices; there's just no way to successfully cover up an unethical practice of spirituality over the long term. It's essential that the tweaks to public-facing images are well grounded in private dedication to spiritual best practice.

The good news is that a genuine commitment to spiritual best practice is both unstoppable and attractive. We've pointed out that the business literature is grappling with what makes organizations great from both a quantitative and a qualitative research perspective, and shown footnoted examples of somewhat wide-eyed studies that admit spiritual best practices work, so what's stopping you? As you practice personally, you'll notice others' natural curiosity about what you're doing differently. Teach them. Encourage them. If the opportunity appears, mentor them.

Now that you've considered this carefully and tried the exercises to jump-start your practice, does it really seem all that difficult? Here's some contrast to enliven your answer:

- You could either keep track of all the lies you tell various people for a lifetime, or just be **authentic**;

- You could either **manipulate** people to do what you want with threats and coercion, or **manipulate** them with **kindness** and **humor**;

- You could either rule the organization with fear and intimidation, or offer people **appreciation** and **dignity**.

That old-school best practice handbook? Toss it. You have something much better now. And you want to know a surprising fact? There are thousands – perhaps tens of thousands! – of years of evidence that this stuff works, and works well. What are you waiting for?

Welcome to the revolution.

SKEPTICS, CRITICS AND HATERS

Up to now, this book has been forward-focused. We have discussed the use and purpose of **contrast** in a positive light. Nevertheless, it would be naive to ignore the skeptics, critics and haters in the world for whom spiritual best practices are anathema, and in whose organizations books like this one will never become required reading. That's fine, but in **fairness**, it would be a disservice to you, loyal Reader, if we left you defenseless with such fine ideas. Therefore, we will use spiritual best practices to offer a sort of script to deal with such people, and the spiritual practice in use will be obvious as it goes along – you decide which ones are best.

Skeptic, Critic or Hater (SCH): (**disdain**) Hey! You with the spiritual best practice BS! Yeah, you, Bill! (**arrogance**) What gives you the right to spread this stuff all over my organization? (**antagonism**) We're doing just fine, thank you, and we don't need your kind of crystal-crunching mucking up what this team has done so well for so long. (**meanness** & **humor**) What was that Jack Nicholson line from "As Good As It Gets?" Sell crazy somewhere else; we're all stocked up here!

Spiritual Best Practice-r (Bill): (**empathy**) I understand, believe me, because at one time in my limited experience, I felt the same way as you: leave that spiritual stuff in church where it belongs. (**vision**) But does it matter to you that no less an authority than Fortune Knowledge Group has studied this stuff and found compelling results? (**dialogue**) Sure, their terms are like "culture" and "beliefs" and "employee engagement" and "values," but that's just to be politically correct.

SCH: (**fairness**) I'll give you 30 seconds to make your case.

Bill: (**respect**) Fair enough! (**appreciation**) Thank you – I'll get it done in 25. (**equity**) Sixty percent of respondents in the Fortune study said their organizations are trying to do what's right, even if that doesn't maximize revenue, and (let me quote this directly from the Executive Overview):

> "(**ethics**) Eighty-one percent of executives believe that companies that are successful at building long-term relationships make a direct correlation between what they believe in and the way they conduct their business. (**abundance**) An even higher proportion (89%) agrees that great companies build cultures that create excellent customer experiences."

(**integrity**) Finally, 68% of respondents to this worldwide survey agreed that it is worth making short-term sacrifices to cultivate long-term relationships.

(**authenticity**) Those kinds of numbers really got my attention, and helped me get my thoughts written down in this useful book.

SCH: (**loyalty**) Well, while I appreciate those results, they don't really reflect our organization. (**bias**) Plus, I don't like the implied exposure of being politically incorrect. (**disdain**) I mean: "What they believe in?" "Culture?" Come on! (**dialogue**) When have beliefs ever really affected *our* bottom line? (**rigidity**) And our culture works just fine, thank you!

Bill: (**dialogue**) If this is about the word "spirituality," I agree that it's a charged term, but maybe we can agree on the *objective* behind those terms – behind the spiritual best practices themselves – that is, enhancing your organization's success? (**authenticity**) Would you agree that life is, in part, about discovery and realization of our spirit – our essential selves?

SCH: (**cooperation**) Yeah. (**arrogance**) I get *that* on the golf course.

Bill: (**dialogue**) Do you play with people from the office? (**respect**) Do they see you light up when you sink a difficult putt, or get great yardage from a tough lie?

SCH: (**authenticity**) Yeah, I guess they do. It's high fives all around for stuff like that.

Bill: (**empathy** & **dialogue**) And do you offer high fives all around at the office when your team makes a tough deadline or exceeds an objective?

SCH: (**discretion**) Well…sometimes…that's not really how things roll around this office!

Bill: (**vision**) What we're really discussing is how to build a fire in the belly of every one of your team members – a fire that *you*, my friend, can start… *and* that you won't have to keep stoking, because this stuff is contagious and self-evident once it gets started. (**courage**) The buzz these days is "employee engagement," and doesn't your organization want to maximize that?

SCH: (**dialogue** & **bias**) I heard the people in human resources talking about employee engagement, but they aren't going to like this spiritual stuff…still has too many religious overtones. (**inconsistency**) And I'm not certain high fives all the time are good for office decorum. (**arrogance**) This is a tight ship and I don't take crap from anyone.

Bill: (**compromise**) May I suggest something, if it's OK with you? (**cooperation**) Why don't we give a few of your team leaders a copy of this book and an assignment to come back in a month with concrete plans for how it could be implemented in their teams? (**deliberation**) Let them explain how and if it could mesh with your organization. (**collaboration**) If HR wants to ring in on the process, let them join in, too. (**respect**) Then you decide if it's worthwhile.

SCH: (**authenticity** & **inconsistency**) Well Bill, I'm still skeptical, but I'm always willing to listen to my team's opinions. (**cooperation**) If they have questions, can they contact you? (**dissent**) And believe me, this goes *nowhere* if there's not a clear advantage to us!

Bill: (**equity**) Sure, hit me any time. (**humility**) If I don't have all the answers I will research your questions and bring you the best responses I can find.

SCH: (**discretion**) Let's keep the project just between you, me, and my team leads for now, OK? (**arrogance**) And if they nix it, no harm no foul…but what's in it for me if the team wants to give spiritual best practicing a try?

Bill: (**humor**) You mean even more success isn't enough? (**equity**) How about I give you some space in the front of the book to write a recommendation?

SCH: (**disrespect**) Bill, you're lucky you got your point across in 30 seconds or we wouldn't still be talking. (**agitation**) Care to make this interesting?

Bill: (**resilience**) What do you have in mind?

SCH: (**equity**) If – and I mean *if* – the team wants to move forward, I'll write that recommendation for your book, but I want to give a bunch of signed copies to my friends – maybe 50?

Bill: (**empathy**) So, let me get this straight: your team leads recommend it, and you order it, and the entire organization adopts spiritual best practices just like that, and all I've got to do is give you 50 signed copies of the book for your peers? (**humor**) I've got that many in my car right now!

SCH: (**integrity**) Not with my recommendation printed in them you don't! (**compromise**) Plus, it's going to take us at least two months to work this into the schedule, and 30-45 days after that to get the team leads engaged. Deal?

Bill: (**appreciation**) Thank you for taking your time to discuss this. Much appreciated. (shakes *SCH*'s hand).

SCH: (**carelessness**) Call you in a few months.

Bill: (**contrast**) You'll hear from me first!

———————

From this conversation, can you see that much of what we say every day connects to some form of spiritual practice? Do you understand that, by responding mainly to the spiritual best practices *SCH* offered me, and even offering empathy and respect for *SCH*'s not-so-good ones, I was able to lead the conversation in a beneficial direction? This is the essence of spiritual best practice in relationship; even when that relationship is slightly antagonistic, it's still possible to achieve a mutual objective.

As promised in the discussion of politics, this little script also illustrates the skillful **manipulation** of **discourse** so that the people holding opposing viewpoints didn't get into a shouting match. *SCH* revealed quite a bit about the spiritual practices behind his viewpoint, and when one of those practices hit the "best" button, it was met with **dialogue**. *SCH* was **consistent** about the persona he chose to put on display, which seemed to be **authentic** in many ways: who hasn't had a manager that's a bit **biased**, **arrogant**, and **inflexible**? But that doesn't have to stop the exchange.

Did this conversation with *SCH* achieve **equity**? Both parties worked hard to get to a deal both could accept without harm to either one, and their agreement seemed doable to each. The tip-off for **equity** is this sort of willingness; each party recognizes the benefit to the other, and undue hardship isn't part of the agreement. Since the exchange didn't deplete non-renewable resources, it's not a tragedy of the commons, and it may well be sustainable: *SCH* will endorse and advance the book for the **fair** exchange of 50 copies, which is non-exploitive. Beyond this, there's no hint of an economic theory at work save for the freedom both parties have to conduct the exchange, which is more capitalist than socialist (without value judgment, please!). Isn't this what truly ought to be meant by "fair trade?"

It's also obvious in the conversation that **contrast** was used to reach agreement, but indirectly. How? By staying consistent with the spiritual best practice, I was able to hold my position opposite *SCH* without losing ground. Had I returned any of *SCH*'s less-than-best spiritual practice in kind, the creative tension of **contrast** may have been lost, and I would have been out the door.

If this material seems simple...well, it ought to be! Isn't it about time to complement all that academic evidence and case study research with self-evident, common sense, reasonable practices? There's no shortage of issues facing organizations, and if the lubrication they need – or have been using – boils down to spiritual best practices that are grounded in thousands of years of successful human culture, what are you waiting for?

Still want to sound off? Email me with your questions. I promise I'll respond. I'll even put the best ones into an online FAQ and include them in subsequent editions of this book. My best teachers have always been my toughest critics, so I welcome you, *SCH* I don't yet know, and I look forward to your insight.

Bill@MusicCare.net

CHAPTER FIVE

FURTHER SUGGESTIONS

HOW TO RECOGNIZE EXISTING SPIRITUAL PROGRAM INITIATIVES

Organizations may employ spiritual best practices enter-prise-wide or with a specific initiative or program. A global corporation or a government agency, for example, may be too large to engage spiritual best practices across the board – as much as that might help! – but could successfully do so on a program/initiative level.

It's easy to recognize programs in "spiritual" crisis because they make the news: America's universal health care program; wounded warriors struggling with "moral injury;" questions around the proper use of nuclear energy. One of my recent favorites is the failure of some software coding initiatives to account properly for racial, gender or social class bias – the so-called "human" factor. There's much more about that last one in an excellent arti-cle from Wired,[32] which the following excerpt highlights famously:

> "Microsoft's CEO [Satya Nadella] was once asked,
> in a technical interview, what he would do if he saw

a baby lying in an intersection: the obvious answer to pick up the baby did not occur to him."

It can be difficult to remember that, as excellent as our approach to a particular issue may be, and as sound as the underlying research may be, there's always a human factor to engage successfully if the program itself is to be successful. This book suggests that doing this works best through spiritual best practices, and we are about to see real-life examples of why that's so.

First, how do we recognize spiritual best practices in program initiatives? It's very much like identifying them in organizations. Recall that these, and perhaps others, are truisms about spiritual best practices:

- It's possible to learn the spiritual practice at work by examining the language used to communicate it (that is, "compassion" speaks of spiritual best practice while "coercion" doesn't). Going beyond the mission statement to the program description, for example, is a good way to make this evaluation. In smaller organizations, such as families or work groups, is there a shared, written statement or purpose for the program? Our family has regular meetings to discuss and set expectations, and we write them down with an eye to what's age-appropriate and doable for each of us to achieve. This is done with the expectation that what helps each one of us is best for all of us, which is an excellent spiritual best practice!

- It's possible to discover spiritual best practices by watching the actions of an organization as it does business: are people engaged, eager, knowledgeable, skillful communicators? If so, there's a good chance spiritual best practices are in play. If possible, give yourself or your team some advanced education by visiting your customers or suppliers at their places of business to observe and learn about the way they achieve success. If the "how" isn't as obvious as the "why," ask good questions and pay close attention to the answers! This process works equally well when applied to a program, such as feeding homeless people. Observe and ask questions such as these: what's the demeanor of the program workers actually doing the work?; how are the clients responding to the program workers?; when difficulties arise, how are they resolved: with spiritual best practices or not?

- The lazy approach to discover spiritual best practices at work in an organization is to read online reviews: what do people who interact with the organization say about it? Praise? Criticism? If you work with the organization being reviewed – or if it's your own organization! – the reviewers' language will often synchronize with the organization's embrace of spiritual practice in an obvious way, whether bad or good.

Here are three successful program initiatives you may recognize. As we investigate each one, use the skills you've learned from this book to decide for yourself whether spiritual best practices are in use. We will keep it simple and (mostly) avoid the thorny issues of war, nuclear energy and humanities-inflected software!

Of course, it's possible to have successful program initiatives that have nothing to do with spiritual best practices. Examples could include many viral videos, such as those highlighting someone's amazing talent, or a raunchy celebrity exposé – there's popularity in rising above the noise, but it's rare that video does so with such alacrity and implied spiritual best practice as the recent Heineken ad we'll consider first.

Heineken: 'Worlds Apart' Experiment[33]

What it is: A video advertisement for Heineken beer that suggests a way forward when opposing viewpoints are in contention.

The Setup: Two people with opposing opinions discuss their points of view over a beer.

The Catch: Before the big reveal ("You *don't* share the same beliefs as me?") they get to know one another doing brief cooperative tasks and engaging in meaningful dialogue.

The Point: It's harder to hate someone you know…in fact, it's possible to actually relate well with someone who holds a radically different viewpoint from yours.

How it is spiritual best practice: **Dialogue** with **empathy** and **compassion**.

Discussion: Clearly, there's a sense of the dramatic in this 'experiment:' by the time the two people in each dyad find out that they have very different opinions about their topic, they have gotten to know each other as human beings. After the reveal, each dyad chooses to keep talking rather than turn away. That's the result of spiritual best practices at work.

If you missed any of the spiritual best practices, the ad actually spells each of them out for you:

- Two strangers meet for the first time – **acceptance**

- Each knows nothing about the other – **humility**

- Or what this experiment involves – **fairness**

- Is there more that unites us than divides us? – **contrast**

- The Icebreaker – **courage**

- Q&A – **dialogue**

- Bridge Building – **cooperation**

- The Decision – **authenticity** and **engagement**

Questions to ask:

- Does it matter whether or not these were real people or actors?

- What mattered more in this ad: spiritual best practice terms or spiritual best practice actions?

Our second example comes from the social services sector, specifically homeless military Veterans services. A good idea that got started in one city in the late 1980s has spontaneously blossomed into more than 200 annual events nationwide in 2016. Something must be going right!

Stand Down

"Stand Downs are typically one- to three-day events providing supplies and services to homeless Veterans, such as food, shelter, clothing, health screenings and VA Social Security benefits counseling. Veterans can also receive referrals to other assistance such as health care, housing solutions, employment, substance use treatment and mental health counseling. They are collaborative events, coordinated between local VA Medical Centers, other government agencies and community-based homeless service providers."[34]

The first Stand Down took place in San Diego, California, in 1988. At this writing, there are more than 200 Stand Down events throughout the United States each year.

The Setup: Government, public and private resources are pooled to create a temporary tent city where homeless Veterans may receive care, services and support.

The Catch: For those who want to, Veterans are encouraged to take steps out of homelessness, but it's not a requirement to do so in order to receive services and supplies – it's not uncommon for formerly homeless Veterans to return to Stand Down as volunteers.

The Point: Homeless military Veterans deserve better than life on the streets; after all, they pledged their lives in service to their country.

How it is spiritual best practice: **Dignity** with **compassion** and **respect, honor, appreciation** and **altruism**; **cooperation** and **collaboration**.

Questions to ask:

- What motivates "local VA Medical Centers, other government agencies and community-based homeless service providers" put on more than 200 of these events every year? Do the math: that's more than 1,000 organizations cooperating! Every year! How is this possible?

- Are Stand Downs **sustainable**? Why or why not?

We've seen how for-profit and not-for-profit program initiatives can successfully embody spiritual best practices. Now let's look at a successful government program that does so, with close attention to how this program fits into economic spiritual best practices.

The Public Library System

Yes, your public library is one of the government's most successful programs, and it's a model of spiritual best practices. The public library system isn't perfect, of course, and the issues it faces are salient ones. But it has a history of success that's instructive as we consider what a successful government program might look like, including identifying and effectively addressing a large-scale societal need (literacy), operating revenue-positive (or even revenue-neutral!), and leveraging its many assets well.

We are going to approach this example from a slightly different standpoint: the financial one. Here is a quick summary the most-recently available financial facts (2012), published in 2014, for US public libraries:[35]

- The public library system cost around $10.7 billion in 2012, and had revenue of $11.5 billion;

- About 85% of funding comes from the local communities the libraries serve – only 7% of funding comes from state or federal grants;

- Staff is the biggest single expense for public libraries, amounting to 68% of total costs;

- There were 1.5 billion visits to public libraries in fiscal year 2012, with an average of 8 books borrowed per unique patron.

How does all that reflect spiritual best practices? And aren't public libraries an anachronism in these days of instant online access to everything?

First of all, the public library system is a government program that's revenue positive. For a bit less than $40 per year (paid through tax revenue and other invisibly painless methods of obtaining funds from you and me), anyone living in the United States can have unlimited age-appropriate "free" access to books, periodicals, information (including the Internet of course), and related services. Yes, it takes a lot of effort for libraries to raise and retain those funds and yes, library staffers are likely very underpaid for their skills. So what makes this work so well? Skillful management? Dedicated fundraising? Volunteers?

Do you remember a librarian who may have influenced your life when you were a kid? Honestly, I don't, but I have a very positive memory of our local library. Mom took me to visit the library many times when I was in preschool and elementary school. There were reading groups staffed by volunteers. There were some pretty scary people behind the big counter where I was given my first library card, and I learned how to borrow books and bring them back on time (possibly through intimidation!). I learned what late fees were and how to avoid them. I remember checking out stacks of books almost too heavy to carry. As a little kid, these were some of my first lessons in economics.

Yes: economics. Here are three important points any kid can learn simply by using a library's circulation system:

- A library provides common goods (books and information are rivalrous, and "free" access to them is non-excludable);

- **Equity** is extended to all borrowers;

- A library manages **scarcity** by assessing late fees.

Those basic economics lessons I learned are a big part of how the library system does business with its patrons. Simple. Easy to understand. Effective. For **contrast**, try to check out a book from your local college or university library! There are other factors involved there, and you may quickly find that the same **equity** extended to you through the public library system may not follow you to the temples of higher learning…unless you have the proper credentials, of course. Need further proof of how well the public library works? Visit one, and use its "free" Internet service to figure out how well your State Department of Motor Vehicles works and what you, as a driver or license holder, actually gain from participating in that system! The economics aren't quite as easy to understand, nor are they as compelling, but you may find the **contrast** between the two government programs instructive.

In spite of their scary appearance, I also remember the staff at our local library being very **kind** and **appreciative** whenever I'd return the books I'd borrowed, even if I had to pay a late fee, but that might have been a sign of those times. Although that sort of warm, welcoming demeanor hasn't marked my adult visits to libraries, my perspective has also grown up with me – we're not looking for perfection here, just spiritual best practices. And, the library staff is *always* much more helpful than anyone I've ever found across the counter at the DMV.

Back to those financials....

It's noteworthy that public libraries receive the majority of their operating funds from the local communities they serve, not from the State or Federal government. This is an important lesson for those concerned with economics: local funding and local control of common goods works very well for libraries. Could this be why libraries have enjoyed a measure of successful **sustainability**? (There will be a question to ponder about this point at the end of the section.)

What about the people who take time out of their day to read to kids at the public library? Whether staffers or volunteers, can we agree that reading to kids is a good thing? Isn't this exchange on a spiritual best practices level? A commitment to serve, especially as a volunteer or underpaid staffer, indicates some level of **altruism** and devotion to **sustainability** doesn't it? A literate population benefits everyone, and the **vision** of the public library system is precisely that.

While we could make cost-based statements about the impact of libraries on literacy, the measure of a library's **sustainability** goes far beyond its cost to those intangible "in kind" services it gives and receives from its local community, and even to the overall benefit of a literate public, doesn't it? Of course, people learn to read in many different ways, but there would be a gap in the fabric of literacy without the public library system and the **loyalty** of the people and resources dedicated to it. If we could fully pay those staffers for the results they have produced, what would that payment be? How would we even calculate it? Could we – the public – even afford it?

I hope that considering the value of library staff strengthens your understanding of this spiritual best practices truism:

> *The value of a spiritual best practice is often far in excess of its monetary measure.*

The obverse statement is a bit frightening, because it requires us to imagine a world in which library staffers, for example, could be paid based on the value of their work to society as a whole (improved literacy). One of the only ways to calculate that value would be to suppose a higher level of illiteracy and the cost to an entire population of the various negative results that brings. A necessary part of the human trajectory through history includes our ability to look back at how things have been done, and at our historical failures and successes; perhaps underpaid library staffers and volunteers persist in their mission because they've had time to read some of that history, and have the **courage** to envision what the world might be like without them and the libraries they serve.

One of the big issues facing public libraries today is encouraging more patrons to visit more frequently. A billion and a half visits per year seems like a lot, but that's for a population of some 330 million people, most of whom don't use the public library system...and the number of annual visits has been declining over the last few years. Clearly, the need for and use of any given library is a function of the local demographic it serves, and this is perhaps the biggest reason for libraries' funding and control to reside at the local level: local communities generally understand their needs better than a distant politician or committee can.

The public library system has been challenged by the availability of online access to information. It is adapting to this in locally-appropriate ways, which demonstrates another spiritual best practice we will mention here for the first time: **flexibility**. Through these changes, we can also observe **resilience** of the system and **loyalty** of the funding resources.

Here in San Diego, our local libraries are responding to social needs through **collaboration** with government and private agencies to become hubs of community resources, offering homeless people **dignity**, hungry people **compassion**, and distressed, stressed and anxious people **patience** and **kindness**, even if that only means a comfortable chair in which to relax for a few minutes. Those things have little to do with circulation (checking out books), but they have everything to do with the needs of our community, and if a library can be a community oasis isn't that a good thing?

Questions to ask:

- Is the public library system a socialist or capitalist economic engine? In what way(s) does this matter?

- Are there other common goods where local funding and local control might work better than State or Federal funding and control?

- What trade-offs exist between the value of a spiritual best practice and the revenue that might result from it?

- Would public libraries be more cost-effective if funding and management for them was centralized? How would that look in practice? What would this mean for local, community-based services and resources that might be eliminated "to save money?"

- How does the public library system serve as a model for a sustainable spiritual best practices program?

Now, let us consider how to build a program initiative that incorporates spiritual best practices.

HOW TO TO CREATE SPECIFIC SPIRITUAL PROGRAM INITIATIVES

Building a program from scratch gives us the chance to incorporate spiritual best practices right from the start, although it's a fact that organizations tend to naturally offer programs (and products) that reflect their internal practices, whether spiritual best or not. This how-to example must be quite general, but if we begin with the right sorts of assumptions, it can apply to almost any program initiative. By this time, you're familiar with the basics, so it's quite possible you're already a few steps ahead. That's fine. Well done!

To begin, may we make the assumption that you or your organization are already skillful spiritual best practitioners, or are now well on your way? It's a fair assumption, even if it's still just an aspiration, because spiritual best practices tend to be contagious once they are introduced, so let us blithely proceed to do so and trust that the process will carry the day. Fair enough?

The Objective

The first question to ask is also the easiest to answer: what's your program objective? Feed one hundred homeless people each week? Create a mobile game that's revenue-positive by the end of the year? Improve time-to-resolution in the customer care center within three months? Get the kids to do chores more willingly NOW? Grab something to write on and write it down. Make sure it is *measureable!* Here's a sample:

Within the next _____ days/weeks/months, I/we will:

_____

_____

_____

and success means that:

_____

_____

_____

With me so far?

The How

If you're building a program from scratch, you already know the "why" (help end hunger among homeless people; earn money from online gaming; happier customers; a cleaner house). Incorporating spiritual best practices, as you now know, is all about the "how." So the next questions help focus the "how" around spiritual best practices. Write down as many actionable steps as you can think of that might help achieve the objective. Do this without making a value judgment about whether any of them might work better or worse. Yes: this is old-fashioned brainstorming, but stay with me!

Now it's time to incorporate spiritual best practices.

Let's assume for a moment that your objective is feeding one hundred homeless people each week, and that your list of action steps includes items about how to find the funding you will need, staff the paid employees and volunteers, obtain the food, transport and store it, where and how to set up the buffet, and how to engage the homeless people you wish to serve. It's a big undertaking, and clearly a useful one.

If feeding homeless people is already within your skill-set, there's a good chance you've got extremely concrete and organized plans; if you are new to the task, there will be things you miss – this is all OK! Whether you are doing this exercise "for real" or as a skill-building example, you will get results from the process.

Here's how to incorporate the "how." It's easy:

> *For each task on your brainstormed list, ask the question: Which specific spiritual best practice(s) can be engaged in this task?*

For example, one of your tasks might be "collect leftover, edible food from local restaurants." (There's already at least one tax-advantaged not-for-profit organization doing this!) There's a lot of logistics packed into that task; what we want to discover is the spiritual best practice "how." Here are a few ideas:

- We **collaborate** with local restaurants to obtain suitable food that can be transported and stored without spoiling;

- We offer tangible **appreciation** for the food we obtain;

- We are **patient** with our local restaurant "suppliers," and show **respect** for their ability to participate at whatever level of contribution they can make;

- We offer **equity** to our local restaurant "suppliers" by extending publicity for them within our own promotional materials.

Do you see the ways in which these spiritual best practices inflect the process? Just to remind you of what you've already learned about the underlying research: people and businesses *want* to engage with you when you offer a process that's based in spiritual best practice.

Now, you're ready to incorporate the spiritual best practices in this task. To over-simplify, your to-do item has gone from this:

"Collect leftover, edible food from local restaurants;"

to this:

"**Patiently collaborate** with local restaurants to obtain suitable food that can be transported and stored without spoiling, and offer tangible, **equitable appreciation** in the form of **respectful** restaurant publicity in our own promotional materials in exchange for each restaurant's **generosity**, whatever the amount of the contribution."

It may seem obvious at this point, but, if you were a restaurant owner with an interest in serving your community and an agency approached you to help, which to-do item above would get your attention? Again, the research favors the second, spiritual best practices model.

As you roll through the various steps in your master objective to-do list, you might find some that have nothing to do with spiritual best practices or can't be enhanced to include them. That's an opportunity to consider whether the task is essential to the objective or contributes in any meaningful way to achieving it. For example, you might find that, after everyone has been fed, there's still uneaten, perhaps inedible remaining food. If your original task was "dispose of inedible food" by throwing it away or stuffing it down the Somat, and there's no commercial worm farm or composting operation close by that would benefit from the leavings, you may very well have a task that won't respond to spiritual best practice. We don't want to make the perfect good's enemy! You're doing well to engage in this process; even if it isn't immediately apparent in this exercise, there's a good chance that there's a spiritual best practice or two for each of your tasks.

Yes: it's important to write this stuff down. Here's a secret successful people know: committing new ideas to paper – whether physical or digital – brings their execution in real life that much closer, so please write down your responses to whatever the objective tasks may be that you and/or your team might be considering.

Wrap-up for the "how" phase is easy. It means that you've achieved your spiritual best practice thinking for each brainstormed item in your objective task list and written it down in something like a logical order. This is now your master project task list for accomplishing the objective using spiritual best practices.

The Launch
Doesn't matter if you are doing chores or kicking off a multi-city program initiative; you're standing out from

the competition because you've taken time to do two very important things that immediately set you apart:

1. You actually planned this thing, from start to finish, and have a practical process for achieving the objective (this is where most people and organizations stop!);

and

2. You have purposefully incorporated spiritual best practices into the process (this is what sets you apart!).

You (or your team) are already capable of doing the work, correct? There may be skills you need to learn or hire, but you wouldn't be taking this on unless you (and your team) were up to meeting the objective, so it's time to begin.

We've been taught to "begin with the end in mind," and I've no trouble with that, but this book is all about what happens *after* you begin: the "how." That means, in practice, that you and your team will be getting the work done in a new way (or perhaps a way that already seems familiar), because you will be emphasizing the "how" for every task you accomplish.

To extend our example one step further, the driver who picks up leftover food from restaurants is going to show **patience**, **appreciation**, and **respect** for the restaurant's **generosity**…*every time that driver has the opportunity to* *do so.* Sure, it's fine to send a computer-generated note of thanks, but *spiritual best practices live and work inside human connection*, so your driver needs to **authentically** practice these spiritual bests. Every time. With every restaurant employee the driver engages. At every restaurant. This ups the ante on excellence in ways you can't even imagine. Yes: it's wont work if it's **fake** or **coerced** or **insincere**, so that driver had better be the right person for the job! Agreed?

The example here is meant to be an intuitive "just makes sense" model for real life practice. A nod to the haters (SCH, are you listening?): If there's a reason you need to **resist** these ideas, I've no issue with that. There are plenty of people and teams and organizations who already do the spiritual best practice thing; this book's purpose is to make that doing tangible and scalable in ways people and organizations can use to set themselves apart, attract opportunity, connect more authentically, grow and thrive. Prove these ideas for yourself...or not. They aren't going away.

Three... two... one... Launch!

The Example

My friend and colleague, Rob Reider, has written a novel that actually describes, in detail, the inception, development, and launch of a community-based social change organization. It's called "American Scream – A Novel of Hope and Possibilities." Careful readers will notice it has been mentioned here before. It's part of the reason this book came into being. I encourage you to take a few hours to engage with it, not as a fictional novel (which it is) but as a detailed description of hopeful possibility – the possibility of what could happen, given the right sort of circumstances.

No single essay or book can do complete justice to the leaders and ideas on whose shoulders it rests. For that reason, I want to encourage you to put some of these on your short list of stuff to read. (The implication is that you will also include these next time you visit the pipeline at Web Beach...surf's up!) Enjoy!

- *The Miracle in Front of You* – an interview with Raymond Barfield on Practicing Medicine with Compassion" published in "The Sun," January 2016[36]

- Robert K Greenleaf: *Servant Leadership: A Journey into the Nature of Legitimate Power and Greatness*[37]

- National Mentoring Resource Center[38]

- Love and Logic[39] resources for parents, teachers and others that incorporate what this book calls spiritual best practices

- "I Am Not Your Guru," a Netflix documentary featuring Tony Robbins

- *American Scream* and *The Genius Club*, novels by Rob Reider[40]

- Daniel C. Dennett: *Consciousness Explained*[41]

ENDNOTES

1   Sweeny, Patrick and Pargament, Kenneth: *Building Spiritual Fitness in the Army – An Innovative Approach to a Vital Aspect of Human Development*, American Psychologist, January 2011

2   See http://www.businessinsider.com/ibms-cult-like-songbook-from-1937-2014-8 accessed March 2017

3   See https://qz.com/2330/hail-to-the-ibm-and-other-corporate-anthems-to-sing-along-to/ accessed March 2017

4   http://apps.who.int/gb/ebwha/pdf_files/EB130/B130_9-en.pdf accessed January 2017

5   https://sammysoap.com/#mission accessed January 2017

6   https://www.nytimes.com/2015/11/03/health/death-rates-rising-for-middle-aged-white-americans-study-finds.html?_r=0 accessed January 2017

7   See http://www.who.int/mental_health/management/depression/wfmh_paper_depression_wmhd_2012.pdf accessed January 2017

8   Reider, Rob: *American Scream: A Novel of Hope and Possibilities*, American Star Books, 2012 and Reider, Rob: *The Genius Club for*

Survivors Only, A Novel of Life and Survival in Declining America, Rowe Publishing, 2016

9   http://globalnews.amway.com/facts accessed January 2017

10 https://youtu.be/HUHMZf3qwsQ for official trailer accessed January 2017

11 See https://www.ncbi.nlm.nih.gov/pmc/articles/PMC2352144/ accessed March 2017: "Does Mentoring Matter? A Multi-Disciplinary Meta-Analysis Comparing Mentored and Non-Mentored Individuals," Eby, Allen, Evans, Ng and DuBois, US National Library of Medicine, National Institutes of Health, 2008

12 Available at https://www.gyro.com/beyondthebrand/ accessed February 2017 Executive Summary page 5

13 Available at https://www.bostonglobe.com/magazine/2015/11/10/the-surprising-power-being-nice-your-employees/yiEkkCB6hN3GSdKZOn2KyK/story.html accessed February 2017

14 Available at https://www.entrepreneur.com/article/251089 accessed February 2015

15 Available at https://www.researchgate.net/publication/49740671_Building_Spiritual_Fitness_in_the_Army_An_Innovative_Approach_to_a_Vital_Aspect_of_Human_Development accessed February 2017

16 See https://www.gyro.com/beyondthebrand/ accessed February 2017 Executive Summary page 10

17 See https://en.wikipedia.org/wiki/Madoff_investment_scandal accessed March 2017

18 See http://www.appreciationatwork.com accessed February 2017

19 Schwartz, Tony: "Why Appreciation Matters So Much," Harvard Business Review, January 23, 2012, see https://hbr.org/2012/01/why-appreciation-matters-so-mu accessed February 2017

20 Op cit https://www.bostonglobe.com/magazine/2015/11/10/the-surprising-power-being-nice-your-employees/yiEkkCB6hN3GSdKZOn2KyK/story.html accessed February 2017

21 See https://en.wikipedia.org/wiki/Common_good_(economics) accessed February 2017

22 The four main types of goods are private goods, common pool resources, club goods, and public goods.

Private Goods: An economic good, or a tangible item that can be purchased and traded within a market. Private goods are excludable. They are also rival, or subtractable. You can't eat a hamburger that is being eaten by someone else. For example: Most goods that are commonly traded, from hamburgers to furniture to 747 airplanes.

Club Goods: Goods that are excludable but non-rival, or non-subtractable. This means that while certain people can be excluded from the consumption of a good, one person's consumption of it does not diminish another person's.

For example: Community services, including those provided by religious organizations; cable television; computer software.

Common-Pool Resources: Fisheries, forests, oil fields, groundwater basins, and so on.

Public Goods: National defense, public parks, street lighting, lighthouses, and so on.

Excerpted from: http://www.econport.org/content/handbook/commonpool/cprtable.html accessed February 2017

23 http://nypost.com/2015/08/04/exec-who-set-70k-minimum-wage-learns-tough-lesson/ accessed March 2017

24 See https://en.wikipedia.org/wiki/Self-help#Statistics accessed March 2017

25 See https://www.strategicmanagementinsight.com/mission-statements.html accessed March 2017

26 See https://www.woundedwarriorproject.org/mission accessed March 2017

27 See http://www.directory-online.com/Rotary/accounts/6860/Pages/Global_Scholar_Packet/Appendix_3_-_Mission_Statements_and_Mottoes_of_Rotary_International_and_The_Rotary_Foundation.pdf accessed March 2017

28 See http://sdvetscoalition.org/about-sdvc/ accessed March 2017

29 See https://www.wired.com/2017/04/want-play-scrabble-like-pro-heres-memory-trick/ accesses April 2017

30 Op cit https://www.gyro.com/beyondthebrand/ accessed March 2017 Executive Summary pages 7 and 9

31 Op cit https://www.gyro.com/beyondthebrand/ accessed March 2017 Executive Summary pages 5, 8, and 10

32 See https://www.wired.com/2017/04/hey-computer-scientists-stop-hating-humanities/ accessed April 2017

33 See https://www.youtube.com/watch?v=8wYXw4K0A3g accessed April 2017

34 See https://www.va.gov/homeless/events.asp

35 See https://www.imls.gov/assets/1/AssetManager/PLS_FY2012.pdf accessed April 2017

36 See http://thesunmagazine.org/issues/481/the_miracle_in_front_of_you

37 See https://www.amazon.com/Servant-Leadership-Legitimate-Greatness-Anniversary/dp/0809105543

38 See http://www.mentoring.org/program-resources/national-mentoring-resource-center/

39 See https://www.loveandlogic.com/ accessed May 2017

40 Op cit: Reider, Rob: *American Scream: A Novel of Hope and Possibilities*, American Star Books, 2012 and Reider, Rob: *The Genius Club for Survivors Only, A Novel of Life and Survival in Declining America*, Rowe Publishing, 2016

41 See https://www.amazon.com/Consciousness-Explained-Daniel-C-Dennett/dp/0316180661 accessed May 2017

www.ingramcontent.com/pod-product-compliance
Lightning Source LLC
Chambersburg PA
CBHW071844200326
41519CB00016B/4227